ITALIAN RECIPES 2022

ESSENTIAL AND DELICIOUS RECIPES OF THE REGIONAL TRADITION

ALEX DRAGHI

TABLE OF CONTENTS

Spinach and Potato Gnocchi 10

Seafood Gnocchi with Tomato and Olive Sauce 14

Green Gnocchi in Pink Sauce 18

Semolina Gnocchi 21

Abruzzese Bread Dumplings 23

Ricotta-Filled Crepes 26

Abruzzese Crepe and Mushroom Timbale 29

Tuscan Handmade Spaghetti with Meat Sauce 33

Pici with Garlic and Bread Crumbs 36

Semolina Pasta Dough 38

Cavatelli with Ragù 40

Cavatelli with Calamari and Saffron 42

Cavatelli with Arugula and Tomato 45

Orecchiette with Pork Ragù 47

Orecchiette with Broccoli Rabe 49

Orecchiette with Cauliflower and Tomatoes 51

Orecchiette with Sausage and Cabbage 53

Orecchiette with Swordfish 55

White Risotto 63

Saffron Risotto, Milan Style 66

Asparagus Risotto 69

Risotto with Red Peppers 72

Tomato and Arugula Risotto 75

Risotto with Red Wine and Radicchio 78

Risotto with Creamy Cauliflower 81

Lemon Risotto 84

Spinach Risotto 86

Golden Squash Risotto 89

Venetian Risotto with Peas 91

Springtime Risotto 93

Risotto with Tomatoes and Fontina 96

Shrimp and Celery Risotto 98

Risotto with "Fruits of the Sea" 102

"Sea and Mountain" Risotto 105

Black Risotto 107

Crisp Risotto Pancake 111

Butter Rings 113

Lemon Knots 115

Spice Cookies 118

Wafer Cookies 120

Sweet Ravioli 123

"Ugly-but-Good" Cookies 126

Jam Spots 128

Double-Chocolate Nut Biscotti 130

Chocolate Kisses 133

No-Bake Chocolate "Salame" 136

Prato Biscuits 138

Umbrian Fruit and Nut Biscotti 140

Lemon Nut Biscotti 143

Walnut Biscotti 145

Almond Macaroons 147

Pine Nut Macaroons 150

Hazelnut Bars 152

Walnut Butter Cookies 154

Rainbow Cookies 156

Christmas Fig Cookies 160

Almond Brittle 164

Sicilian Nut Rolls 166

Sponge Cake 169

Citrus Sponge Cake 171

Lemon Olive-Oil Cake 174

Marble Cake 176

Rum Cake 179

Grandmother's Cake 182

Apricot Almond Cake 186

Summer Fruit Torte 189

Autumn Fruit Torte 191

Polenta and Pear Cake 193

Ricotta Cheesecake 196

Sicilian Ricotta Cake 198

Ricotta Crumb Cake 201

Easter Wheat-Berry Cake 204

Chocolate Hazelnut Cake 209

Chocolate Almond Cake 213

Chocolate Orange Torte 216

Spinach and Potato Gnocchi

Gnocchi di Patate e Spinaci

Makes 6 servings

Though it is not often done in Italy, I sometimes like to serve gnocchi with a stew or pot roast. They soak up the sauce nicely and are a nice change from mashed potatoes or polenta. Try these gnocchi (without the sauce and cheese) as an accompaniment to <u>Roman-Style Oxtail Stew</u> or <u>Friuli-Style Beef Stew</u>.

1½ pounds baking potatoes

1 (10-ounce) bag of spinach, trimmed

Salt

2 cups all-purpose flour, plus more for shaping the gnocchi

1 large egg, beaten

    ½ cup <u>Butter and Sage Sauce</u>

1 cup freshly grated Parmigiano-Reggiano

1. Place the potatoes in a large pot with cold water to cover. Cover the pot and bring to a simmer. Cook until the potatoes are tender when pierced with a knife, about 20 minutes.

2. Place the spinach in a large pot with 1/2 cup of water and salt to taste. Cover and cook until the spinach is tender, about 2 to 3 minutes. Drain the spinach and let cool. Place the spinach in a towel and squeeze out the liquid. Very finely chop the spinach.

3. While the potatoes are still warm, peel them and cut them into chunks. Mash the potatoes using the smallest holes of a ricer or food mill, or by hand with a potato masher. Add the spinach, egg, and 2 teaspoons of salt. Stir in 1 1/2 cups of the flour just until blended. The dough will be stiff.

4. Scrape the potatoes onto a floured surface. Knead briefly, adding as much of the remaining flour as necessary to make a soft dough, enough so that the gnocchi will hold their shape when cooked but not so much that they become heavy. The dough should be slightly sticky. If you are in doubt, bring a small saucepan of water to a boil and drop in a piece of the dough as a test. Cook until the gnocco rises to the surface. If the dough begins to come apart, add more flour. Otherwise the dough is fine.

5. Set the dough aside for a moment. Scrape the board to remove any dough scraps. Wash and dry your hands, then dust them with flour. Set out one or two large baking pans and dust them with flour.

6. Cut the dough into 8 pieces. Keeping the remaining dough covered, roll one piece into a long rope about $3/4$ inch thick. Cut the rope into $1/2$-inch nuggets.

7. To shape the dough, hold a fork in one hand with the tines pointed down. With the thumb of the other hand, roll each piece of dough over the back of the tines, pressing lightly to make ridges on one side and an indentation on the other. Let the gnocchi drop onto the prepared pans. The pieces should not touch. Repeat with the remaining dough.

8. Refrigerate the gnocchi until ready to cook. (Gnocchi can also be frozen. Place the baking sheets in the freezer for one hour or until firm. Put the gnocchi in a large heavy-duty plastic bag. Freeze up to one month. Do not thaw before cooking.)

9. Prepare the sauce. To cook the gnocchi, bring a large pot of water to a boil. Add salt to taste. Lower the heat so that the water boils gently. Drop about half of the gnocchi into the water. Cook for about 30 seconds after the gnocchi rise to the surface.

Skim the gnocchi from the pot with a slotted spoon, draining the pieces well.

10. Have ready a heated shallow serving bowl. Pour a thin layer of the hot sauce into the bowl. Add the gnocchi and toss gently. Cook the remaining gnocchi in the same way. Spoon on more sauce and sprinkle with cheese. Serve hot.

Seafood Gnocchi with Tomato and Olive Sauce

Gnocchi di Pesce con Salsa di Olive

Makes 6 servings

In Sicily, potato gnocchi are sometimes flavored with sole or another delicate fish. I serve them with a slightly spicy tomato sauce, but a butter and herb sauce would also be delicious. Cheese is not needed on this pasta.

1 pound baking potatoes

¼ cup olive oil

1 small onion, finely chopped

1 garlic clove

12 ounces fillet of sole or other delicate white fish, cut into 2-inch pieces

½ cup dry white wine

Salt and freshly ground black pepper

1 large egg, beaten

About 2 cups all-purpose flour

Sauce

¼ cup olive oil

1 scallion, chopped

2 anchovy fillets

1 tablespoon black olive paste

2 cups peeled, seeded, and chopped fresh tomatoes or drained and chopped canned imported Italian tomatoes

2 tablespoons chopped fresh flat-leaf parsley

Salt and freshly ground black pepper

1. Place the potatoes in a pot with cold water to cover. Bring to a simmer and cook until very tender when pierced with a knife. Drain and let cool.

2. In a medium skillet, cook the onion and garlic in the olive oil for 5 minutes over medium heat until the onion is tender. Add the fish and cook 1 minute. Add the wine, and salt and pepper to taste. Cook until the fish is tender and the liquid is mostly evaporated, about 5 minutes. Let cool, then scrape the contents of the skillet into a food processor or blender. Puree until smooth.

3. Line large pans with foil or plastic wrap. Pass the potatoes through a ricer or food mill into a large bowl. Add the fish puree and the egg. Gradually add the flour and salt to taste to form a slightly sticky dough. Knead briefly until smooth and well blended.

4. Divide the dough into 6 pieces. Keeping the remaining dough covered, roll one piece into a long rope about $3/4$ inch thick. Cut the rope into $1/2$-inch long nuggets.

5. To shape the dough, hold a fork in one hand with the tines pointed down. With the thumb of the other hand, roll each piece of dough over the back of the tines, pressing lightly to make ridges on one side and an indentation on the other. Let the gnocchi drop onto the prepared pans. The pieces should not touch. Repeat with the remaining dough.

6. Refrigerate the gnocchi until ready to cook. (Gnocchi can also be frozen. Place the baking sheets in the freezer for one hour or until firm. Put the gnocchi in a large heavy-duty plastic bag. Freeze up to 1 month. Do not thaw before cooking.)

7. For the sauce, combine the oil with the scallion in a large skillet. Add the anchovy fillets and cook until the anchovies are dissolved, about 2 minutes. Stir in the olive paste, tomatoes, and

parsley. Add salt and pepper and cook until the tomato juices have thickened slightly, 8 to 10 minutes. Spoon half the sauce into a large warm serving bowl.

8. Prepare the gnocchi: Bring a large pot of water to a boil. Add salt to taste. Lower the heat so that the water boils gently. Drop about half of the gnocchi into the water. Cook for about 30 seconds after the gnocchi rise to the surface. Skim the gnocchi from the pot with a slotted spoon, draining the pieces well. Place the gnocchi in the serving bowl. Cook the remaining gnocchi in the same way. Add the remaining sauce and stir gently. Serve immediately.

Green Gnocchi in Pink Sauce

Gnocchi Verdi in Salsa Rossa

Makes 6 servings

I first had these dumplings in Rome, though they are more typical of Emilia-Romagna and Tuscany. They are lighter than potato gnocchi, and the chopped greens give them a surface texture, so there is no need to shape the dumplings on the fork. For a change, try drizzling them with <u>Butter and Sage Sauce</u>.

3 cups <u>Pink Sauce</u>

1 pound spinach, stems removed

1 pound Swiss chard, stems removed

¼ cup water

Salt

2 tablespoons unsalted butter

¼ cup finely chopped onion

1 pound whole or part-skim ricotta

2 large eggs

1½ cups freshly grated Parmigiano-Reggiano

¼ teaspoon ground nutmeg

Freshly ground black pepper

1½ cups all-purpose flour

1. Prepare the sauce. Then, in a large pot, combine the two greens, water, and salt to taste. Cook 5 minutes or until wilted and tender. Drain and let cool. Wrap the greens in a towel and squeeze to extract the liquid. Chop finely.

2. In a medium skillet, melt the butter over medium heat. Add the onion and cook, stirring frequently, until golden, about 10 minutes.

3. In a large bowl, beat together the ricotta, eggs, 1 cup of the Parmigiano-Reggiano, nutmeg, and salt and pepper to taste. Add the onion and chopped greens and mix well. Stir in the flour until well blended. The dough will be soft.

4. Line baking sheets with parchment or wax paper. Dampen your hands with cool water. Scoop up a tablespoonful of the dough. Lightly shape it into a ¾-inch ball. Place the ball on a baking sheet. Repeat with the remaining dough. Cover with plastic wrap and refrigerate until ready to cook.

5. Bring at least 4 quarts of water to a boil. Add salt to taste. Lower the heat slightly. Add half the gnocchi a few at a time. When they rise to the surface, cook 30 seconds longer.

6. Spoon half the hot sauce into a warm serving platter. Remove the gnocchi with a slotted spoon and drain them well. Add them to the platter. Cover and keep warm while you cook the remaining gnocchi in the same way. Spoon on the remaining sauce and cheese. Serve hot.

Semolina Gnocchi

Gnocchi alla Romana

Makes 4 to 6 servings

Be sure to fully cook the semolina with the liquid. If it is undercooked, it tends to melt into a mass instead of keeping its shape when baked. But even if that does happen, it will still taste great.

2 cups milk

2 cups water

1 cup fine semolina

2 teaspoons salt

4 tablespoons unsalted butter

⅔ cup freshly grated Parmigiano-Reggiano

2 egg yolks

1. In a medium saucepan, heat the milk and 1 cup of the water over medium heat until simmering. Stir together the remaining 1 cup water and the semolina. Scrape the mixture into the liquid.

Add the salt. Cook, stirring constantly, until the mixture comes to a boil. Reduce the heat to low and cook, stirring well, for 20 minutes, or until the mixture is very thick.

2. Remove the pot from the heat. Stir in 2 tablespoons of the butter and half of the cheese. Rapidly beat in the egg yolks with a whisk.

3. Lightly moisten a baking sheet. Pour the semolina onto the sheet and spread it to a $1/2$-inch thickness with a metal spatula. Let cool, then cover and chill for one hour or up to 48 hours.

4. Place a rack in the center of the oven. Preheat the oven to 400°F. Butter a 13 × 9 × 2–inch baking dish.

5. Dip a $1^1/2$-inch cookie or biscuit cutter in cool water. Cut out rounds of the semolina and arrange the pieces in the prepared baking dish, overlapping slightly.

6. Melt the remaining 2 tablespoons butter in a small saucepan, and drizzle it over the gnocchi. Sprinkle with remaining cheese. Bake 20 to 30 minutes or until golden brown and bubbling. Let cool 5 minutes before serving.

Abruzzese Bread Dumplings

Polpette di Pane al Sugo

Makes 6 to 8 servings

When I visited the Orlandi Contucci Ponno winery in Abruzzo, I enjoyed a tasting of their outstanding wines, which included both white Trebbiano d'Abruzzo and red Montepulciano d'Abruzzo varieties, as well as several blends. Wines as good as these deserve good food, and our lunch was not disappointing, especially the dumplings made of eggs, cheese, and bread simmered in tomato sauce. Though I had never had them before, a little research showed me that these "meatless meatballs" are also popular in other regions of Italy such as Calabria and Basilicata.

The cook from the winery told me that she made the dumplings with the mollica of the bread—the inside of the bread with crust removed. I make them with the whole loaf. Since the Italian bread I buy here is not as sturdy as bread in Italy, the crust gives the dumplings added structure.

If you plan to make these ahead of time, keep the dumplings and sauce separate until just before serving time so that the dumplings do not drink up too much of the sauce.

1 12-ounce loaf Italian or French bread, cut into 1-inch pieces (about 8 cups)

2 cups cool water

3 large eggs

½ cup grated Pecorino Romano, plus more for serving

¼ cup chopped fresh parsley

1 garlic clove, finely chopped

Vegetable oil for frying

Sauce

1 medium onion, finely chopped

½ cup olive oil

2 (28-ounce) cans imported Italian peeled tomatoes with their juice, chopped

1 tiny dried peperoncino, crumbled, or a pinch of crushed red pepper

Salt

6 fresh basil leaves

1. Cut or tear the bread into tiny bits or grind the bread in a food processor into coarse crumbs. Soak the bread in the water for 20 minutes. Squeeze the bread to remove the excess water.

2. In a large bowl, beat the eggs, cheese, parsley, and garlic with a pinch of salt and pepper to taste. Stir in the crumbled bread and mix very well. If the mixture seems dry, stir in another egg. Mix well. Shape the mixture into balls about the size of a golf ball.

3. Pour enough oil to reach a depth of $1/2$ inch into a large heavy skillet. Heat the oil over medium heat until a drop of the bread mixture sizzles when it is placed in the oil.

4. Add the balls to the skillet and cook, turning carefully, until golden brown on all sides, about 10 minutes. Drain the balls on paper towels.

5. To make the sauce, in a large saucepan, cook the onion in the olive oil over medium heat until tender. Add the tomatoes, peperoncino, and salt to taste. Simmer 15 minutes or until slightly thickened.

6. Add the bread balls and baste them with the sauce. Simmer 15 minutes more. Sprinkle with the basil. Serve with additional cheese.

Ricotta-Filled Crepes

Manicotti

Makes 6 to 8 servings

Though many cooks use tubes of pasta to make manicotti, this is my mother's Neapolitan family recipe, made with crepes. The finished manicotti are much lighter than they would be made with pasta, and some cooks find manicotti easier to make with crepes.

    3 cups <u>Neapolitan Ragù</u>

Crepes

1 cup all-purpose flour

1 cup water

3 eggs

½ teaspoon salt

Vegetable oil

Filling

2 pounds whole or part-skim ricotta

4 ounces fresh mozzarella, chopped or shredded

½ cup freshly grated Parmigiano-Reggiano

1 large egg

2 tablespoons chopped fresh flat-leaf parsley

Freshly ground black pepper to taste

Pinch of salt

½ cup freshly grated Parmigiano-Reggiano

1. Prepare the ragù. Then, in a large bowl, whisk together the crepe ingredients until smooth. Cover and refrigerate 30 minutes or more.

2. Heat a 6-inch nonstick skillet or omelet pan over medium heat. Brush the pan lightly with oil. Holding the pan in one hand, spoon in about $1/3$ cup of the crepe batter. Immediately lift and rotate the pan to completely cover the base with a thin layer of batter. Pour off any excess batter. Cook one minute, or until the edge of the crepe turns brown and begins to lift away from the pan. With your fingers, flip the crepe over and brown lightly on the other side. Cook 30 seconds more or until spotted with brown.

3. Slide the cooked crepe onto a dinner plate. Repeat, making crepes with the remaining batter and stacking them one on top of the other.

4. To make the filling, stir together all of the ingredients in a large bowl until just combined.

5. Spoon a thin layer of the sauce in a 13 × 9 × 2– inch baking dish. To fill the crepes, place about $1/4$ cup of the filling lengthwise on one side of a crepe. Roll the crepe into a cylinder and place it in the baking dish seam-side down. Continue filling and rolling the remaining crepes, placing them close together. Spoon on additional sauce. Sprinkle with cheese.

6. Place a rack in the center of the oven. Preheat the oven to 350°F. Bake 30 to 45 minutes or until the sauce is bubbling and the manicotti are heated through. Serve hot.

Abruzzese Crepe and Mushroom Timbale

Timballo di Scrippelle

Makes 8 servings

A friend whose grandmother came from Teramo in the Abruzzo region used to reminisce about the delicious casserole of crepes layered with mushrooms and cheese that her grandmother made for holidays. Here is a version of that dish I adapted from the book Ricette di Osterie d'Italia, by Slow Food Editore. According to the book, the crepes descended from the elaborate crepe preparations introduced by French cooks in the region in the seventeenth Century.

$2^1/_2$ cups Tuscan Tomato Sauce

Crepes

5 large eggs

$1^1/_2$ cups water

1 teaspoon salt

$1^1/_2$ cups all-purpose flour

Vegetable oil for frying

Filling

1 cup dried mushrooms

1 cup warm water

¼ cup olive oil

1 pound fresh white mushrooms, rinsed and cut into thick slices

1 garlic clove, finely chopped

2 tablespoons fresh flat-leaf parsley

Salt and freshly ground black pepper

12 ounces fresh mozzarella, sliced and torn into 1-inch pieces

1 cup freshly grated Parmigiano-Reggiano

1. Prepare the tomato sauce. In a large bowl, whisk together the crepe ingredients until smooth. Cover and refrigerate 30 minutes or more.

2. Heat a 6-inch nonstick skillet or omelet pan over medium heat. Brush the pan lightly with oil. Holding the pan in one hand, spoon in about ⅓ cup of the crepe batter. Immediately lift and rotate the pan to completely cover the base with a thin layer of batter. Pour off any excess batter. Cook 1 minute, or until the edge of the crepe turns brown and begins to lift away from the pan. With your fingers, flip the crepe over and brown lightly on the other side. Cook 30 seconds more or until spotted with brown.

3. Slide the cooked crepe onto a dinner plate. Repeat making crepes with the remaining batter, stacking them one on top of the other.

4. To make the filling, soak the dried mushrooms in the water for 30 minutes. Remove the mushrooms and reserve the liquid. Rinse the mushrooms under cold running water to removing any grit, paying special attention to the ends of the stems where soil collects. Chop the mushrooms coarsely. Strain the mushroom liquid through a paper coffee filter into a bowl.

5. In a large skillet, heat the oil. Add the mushrooms. Cook, stirring often, until the mushrooms are browned, 10 minutes. Add the garlic, parsley, and salt and pepper to taste. Cook until the garlic is golden, about 2 minutes more. Stir in the dried mushrooms and their liquid. Cook 5 minutes or until most of the liquid has evaporated.

6. Place a rack in the center of the oven. Preheat the oven to 375°F. In a 13 × 9 × 2-inch baking dish, spoon a thin layer of tomato sauce. Make a layer of crepes, overlapping them slightly. Follow with a layer of mushrooms, mozzarella, sauce, and cheese. Repeat the layering, ending with the crepes, sauce, and grated cheese.

7. Bake 45 to 60 minutes or until the sauce is bubbling. Let rest 10 minutes before serving. Cut into squares and serve hot.

Tuscan Handmade Spaghetti with Meat Sauce

Pici al Ragù

Makes 6 servings

Chewy strands of handmade pasta are popular in Tuscany and parts of Umbria, usually sauced with a meat ragù. The pasta is called either pici *or* pinci, *and it derives from the word* appicciata, *meaning "elongated by hand."*

I learned to make these in Montefollonico at a restaurant called La Chiusa, where the cook comes to each table and gives diners a little demonstration on how to make them. These are very easy to make, though time-consuming.

3 cups unbleached all-purpose flour, plus more for shaping the dough

Salt

1 tablespoon olive oil

About 1 cup water

    6 cups <u>Tuscan Meat Sauce</u>

½ cup freshly grated Parmigiano-Reggiano

1. Place the flour and ¹/₄ teaspoon salt in a large bowl and stir to mix. Pour the olive oil into the center. Begin stirring the mixture while slowly adding the water, stopping when the dough begins to come together and form a ball. Remove the dough to a lightly floured surface and knead it until smooth and elastic, about 10 minutes.

2. Shape the dough into a ball. Cover with an overturned bowl and let stand 30 minutes.

3. Sprinkle a large baking pan with flour. Divide the dough into quarters. Work with one quarter of the dough at a time while you keep the remainder covered. Pinch off small pieces about the size of a hazelnut.

4. On a lightly floured surface with your hands outstretched, roll out each piece of dough to form thin strands about ¹/₈ inch thick. Place the strands on the prepared baking sheet with some space between them. Repeat with the remaining dough. Let the pasta dry uncovered about 1 hour.

5. Meanwhile, prepare the sauce. Then, bring 4 quarts of water to a boil in a large pot. Add salt to taste. Add the pici and cook until al dente, tender yet still firm to the bite. Drain and toss the pasta with the sauce in a large warmed bowl. Sprinkle with the cheese and toss again. Serve hot.

Pici with Garlic and Bread Crumbs

Pici con le Briciole

Makes 4 to 6 servings

This dish is from La Fattoria, a quaint lakeside restaurant near the Etruscan town of Chiusi.

>1 pound <u>Tuscan Handmade Spaghetti with Meat Sauce</u>, steps 1 to 6

½ cup olive oil

4 large garlic cloves

½ cup fine dry bread crumbs

½ cup freshly grated Pecorino Romano

1. **Prepare the pasta.** In a skillet large enough to hold all of the pasta, heat the oil over medium-low heat. Lightly crush the garlic cloves and add them to the pan. Cook until the garlic is golden, about 5 minutes. Do not let it become brown. Remove the garlic from the pan and stir in the bread crumbs. Cook, stirring often, until the crumbs are browned, about 5 minutes.

2. Meanwhile, bring at least 4 quarts of water to a boil. Add the pasta and 2 tablespoons of salt. Stir well. Cook over high heat,

stirring frequently, until the pasta is al dente, tender yet firm to the bite. Drain the pasta.

3. Add the pasta to the skillet with the crumbs and toss well over medium heat. Sprinkle with the cheese and toss again. Serve immediately.

Semolina Pasta Dough

Makes about 1 pound

Semolina flour made from hard durum wheat is used to make several types of fresh pasta in southern Italy, especially Puglia, Calabria, and Basilicata. When cooked, these pastas are chewy and work well paired with robust meat and vegetable sauces. The dough is very stiff. It can be kneaded by hand, though it is quite a workout. I prefer to use a food processor or heavy-duty mixer to do the heavy mixing, then knead it briefly by hand to make sure the consistency is just right.

1½ cups fine semolina flour

1 cup all-purpose flour, plus more for dusting

1 teaspoon salt

About ⅔ cup warm water

1. In the bowl of a food processor or heavy-duty stand mixer, stir together the dry ingredients. Gradually add water to make a stiff, nonsticky dough.

2. Turn the dough out onto a lightly floured surface. Knead until smooth, about 2 minutes.

3. Cover the dough with a bowl and let rest 30 minutes. Dust two large baking sheets with flour.

4. Cut the dough into 8 pieces. Work with one piece at a time, keeping the remaining pieces covered with an overturned bowl. On a lightly floured surface, roll one piece of the dough into a long rope about $1/2$ inch thick. Shape the dough into cavatelli or orrecchiette, as described in the [Cavatelli with Ragù](#) recipe.

Cavatelli with Ragù

Cavatelli con Ragù

Makes 6 to 8 servings

Stores and catalogs that specialize in pasta-making equipment often sell a device for making cavatelli. It looks something like an old-fashioned meat grinder. You clamp it to the countertop, insert a rope of dough at one end, turn the crank, and neatly made cavatelli come out the other end. It makes short work of a batch of this dough, but I would not bother with it unless I made cavatelli frequently.

When shaping the cavatelli, work on a wooden or other rough-textured surface. The rough surface will hold the bits of pasta dough, allowing them to be dragged with the knife rather than sliding as they would on a smooth, slick countertop.

> Sausage Ragù or Sicilian Tomato Sauce

1 pound Semolina Pasta Dough prepared through step 4

Salt

1. Prepare the ragù or sauce. Have ready 2 baking sheets dusted with flour.

2. Cut the dough into $1/2$-inch pieces. Hold a small knife with a dull blade and rounded tip with your index finger pressed against the blade of the knife. Flatten each piece of dough, pressing and dragging it slightly so that the dough curls around the tip of the knife to form a shell shape.

3. Spread the pieces on the prepared pans. Repeat with the remaining dough. (If you are not using the cavatelli within an hour, place the pans in the freezer. When the pieces are firm, scoop them into a plastic bag and seal tightly. Do not thaw before cooking.)

4. To cook, bring four quarts of cold water to a boil over high heat. Add the cavatelli and 2 tablespoons of salt. Cook, stirring occasionally, until the pasta is tender yet still slightly chewy.

5. Drain the cavatelli and pour them into a heated serving bowl. Toss with the sauce. Serve hot.

Cavatelli with Calamari and Saffron

Cavatelli con Sugo di Calamari

Makes 6 servings

The slightly chewy texture of calamari complements the chewiness of the cavatelli in this contemporary Sicilian recipe. The sauce gets a smooth, velvety texture from a mixture of flour and olive oil and a lovely yellow color from saffron.

1 teaspoon saffron threads

2 tablespoons warm water

1 medium onion, finely chopped

2 garlic cloves, very finely chopped

5 tablespoons olive oil

1 pound cleaned calamari (squid), cut into ½-inch rings

½ cup dry white wine

Salt and freshly ground black pepper

1 tablespoon flour

1 pound fresh or frozen cavatelli

¼ cup chopped fresh flat-leaf parsley

Extra-virgin olive oil

1. Crumble the saffron into the warm water and set aside.

2. In a skillet large enough to hold all of the pasta, cook the onion and garlic in 4 tablespoons of the oil over medium heat until the onion is lightly golden, about 10 minutes. Add the calamari and cook, stirring, until the calamari are just opaque, about 2 minutes. Add the wine and salt and pepper to taste. Bring to a simmer and cook 1 minute.

3. Stir together the remaining 1 tablespoon oil and the flour. Stir the mixture into the calamari. Bring to a simmer. Add the saffron mixture and cook 5 minutes more.

4. Meanwhile, bring at least 4 quarts of water to a boil. Add the pasta and 2 tablespoons of salt. Stir well. Cook over high heat, stirring frequently, until the pasta is tender but slightly underdone. Drain the pasta, reserving some of the cooking water.

5. Stir the pasta into the skillet with the calamari. Add a little of the reserved cooking water if the mixture seems dry. Stir in the parsley and mix well. Remove from the heat and drizzle with a little extra-virgin olive oil. Serve immediately.

Cavatelli with Arugula and Tomato

Cavatelli con Rughetta e Pomodori

Makes 4 to 6 servings

Arugula is best known as a salad green, but in Puglia it is often cooked, or, as in this recipe, stirred into hot soup or pasta dishes at the last minute so that it just wilts. I love the nutty spicy flavor it adds.

¼ cup olive oil

2 garlic cloves, finely chopped

2 pounds ripe plum tomatoes, peeled, seeded, and chopped, or 1 (28-ounce) can imported Italian peeled tomatoes with their juice

Salt and freshly ground black pepper

1 pound fresh or frozen cavatelli

½ cup grated ricotta salata or Pecorino Romano

1 large bunch of arugula, trimmed and torn into bite-size pieces (about 2 cups)

1. In a skillet large enough to hold all of the ingredients, cook the garlic in the oil over medium heat until lightly golden, about 2 minutes. Add the tomatoes and salt and pepper to taste. Bring the sauce to a simmer and cook until thickened, about 20 minutes.

2. Bring at least 4 quarts of water to a boil. Add the pasta and salt to taste. Stir well. Cook over high heat, stirring frequently, until the pasta is tender. Drain the pasta, reserving some of the cooking water.

3. Stir the pasta into the tomato sauce with half of the cheese. Add the arugula and stir well. Add a little of the reserved cooking water if the pasta seems too dry. Sprinkle with the remaining cheese and serve immediately.

Orecchiette with Pork Ragù

Orecchiette con Ragù di Maiale

Makes 6 to 8 servings

My friend Dora Marzovilla comes from Rutigliano, near Bari. She is an expert pasta maker, and I have learned a lot by watching her. Dora has a special wooden pasta board that is used only for pasta making. Though Dora makes many types of fresh pasta, such as gnocchi, cavatelli, ravioli, and maloreddus—*Sardinian saffron gnocchi—for her family's New York City restaurant, I Trulli, orecchiette are her specialty.*

Making orecchiette is very similar to making cavatelli. The biggest difference is that the pasta shell has a more open dome shape, something like an overturned Frisbee or, in the fanciful Italian imagination, little ears, which is how they got their name.

   1 recipe Semolina Dough

   3 cups Pork Ragù with Fresh Herbs

½ cup freshly grated Pecorino Romano

1. Prepare ragù and dough. Have ready 2 large baking sheets dusted with flour. Cut the dough into ½-inch pieces. Hold a small knife with a dull blade and rounded tip with your index finger pressed against the blade of the knife. Flatten each piece of dough with the tip of the knife, pressing and dragging it slightly so that the dough forms a disk. Invert each disk over the tip of your thumb creating a dome shape.

2. Spread the pieces on the prepared pans. Repeat with the remaining dough. (If you are not using the orecchiette within 1 hour, place the pans in the freezer. When the pieces are firm, scoop them into a plastic bag and seal tightly. Do not thaw before cooking.)

3. Bring at least 4 quarts of water to a boil. Add the pasta and salt to taste. Stir well. Cook over high heat, stirring frequently, until the pasta is al dente, tender yet still firm to the bite. Drain the pasta, reserving some of the cooking water.

4. Add the pasta to the ragù. Add the cheese and stir well, adding some of the reserved cooking water, if the sauce seems too thick. Serve immediately.

Orecchiette with Broccoli Rabe

Orecchiette con Cime di Rape

Makes 4 to 6 servings

This is practically the official dish of Puglia, and nowhere will you find it more delicious. It calls for broccoli rabe, sometimes called rapini, though turnip greens, mustard, kale, or regular broccoli can also be used. Broccoli rabe has long stems and leaves and a pleasantly bitter flavor, though boiling it tames some of the bitterness and makes it tender.

1 bunch broccoli rabe (about 1½ pounds), cut into 1-inch pieces

Salt

⅓ cup olive oil

4 garlic cloves

8 anchovies fillets

Pinch of crushed red pepper

1 pound fresh orecchiette or cavatelli

1. Bring a large pot of water to a boil. Add the broccoli rabe and salt to taste. Cook the broccoli rabe 5 minutes, then drain it. It should still be firm.

2. Dry the pot. Heat the oil with the garlic over medium-low heat. Add the anchovies and red pepper. When the garlic is golden, add the broccoli rabe. Cook, stirring well to coat the broccoli with the oil, until very tender, about 5 minutes.

3. Bring at least 4 quarts of water to a boil. Add the pasta and salt to taste. Stir well. Cook over high heat, stirring frequently, until the pasta is al dente, tender yet still firm to the bite. Drain the pasta, reserving some of the cooking water.

4. Add the pasta to the broccoli rabe. Cook, stirring, for 1 minute or until the pasta is well blended. Add a little of the cooking water if necessary.

Variation: Eliminate the anchovies. Serve the pasta sprinkled with chopped toasted almonds or grated Pecorino Romano.

Variation: Eliminate the anchovies. Remove the casings from 2 Italian sausages. Chop the meat and cook it with the garlic, hot pepper, and broccoli rabe. Serve sprinkled with Pecorino Romano.

Orecchiette with Cauliflower and Tomatoes

Orecchiette con Cavolfiore e Pomodori

Makes 4 to 6 servings

A Sicilian relative taught me to make this pasta, but it is eaten in Puglia, too. If you prefer, substitute grated cheese for the toasted bread crumbs.

$\frac{1}{3}$ cup plus 2 tablespoons olive oil

1 garlic clove, finely chopped

3 pounds plum tomatoes, peeled, seeded, and chopped or 1 (28-ounce) can imported Italian peeled tomatoes, with their juice, chopped

1 medium cauliflower, trimmed and cut into florets

Salt and freshly ground black pepper

3 tablespoons plain dry bread crumbs

2 anchovies, chopped (optional)

1 pound fresh orecchiette

1. In a skillet large enough to hold all of the ingredients, cook the garlic in $1/3$ cup of the olive oil over medium heat until golden.

Add the tomatoes and salt and pepper to taste. Bring to a simmer and cook 10 minutes.

2. Stir in the cauliflower. Cover and cook, stirring occasionally, until the cauliflower is very tender, about 25 minutes. Crush some of the cauliflower with the back of a spoon.

3. In a small skillet, heat the remaining 2 tablespoons of oil over medium heat. Add the bread crumbs and anchovies, if using. Cook, stirring until the crumbs are toasted and the oil is absorbed.

4. Bring at least 4 quarts of water to a boil. Add the pasta and salt to taste. Cook, stirring frequently, until the pasta is al dente, tender yet still firm to the bite. Drain the pasta, reserving a little of the cooking water.

5. Toss the pasta with the tomato and cauliflower sauce. Add a little of the cooking water if needed. Sprinkle with the bread crumbs and serve immediately.

Orecchiette with Sausage and Cabbage

Orecchiette con Salsiccia e Cavolo

Makes 6 servings

When my friend Domenica Marzovilla returned from a trip to Tuscany, she described to me this pasta that she had eaten at the home of a friend. It sounded so simple and good, I went home and made it.

2 tablespoons olive oil

8 ounces sweet pork sausages

8 ounces hot pork sausages

2 cups canned imported Italian tomatoes, drained and chopped

Salt

1 pound Savoy cabbage (about $\frac{1}{2}$ medium head)

1 pound fresh orecchiette or cavatelli

1. **In a medium saucepan, heat the oil over medium heat. Add the sausages and cook until browned on all sides, about 10 minutes.**

2. Add the tomatoes and a pinch of salt. Bring to a simmer and cook until the sauce is thickened, about 30 minutes.

3. Cut the core from the cabbage. Cut the cabbage into thin strips.

4. Bring a large pot of water to a boil. Add the cabbage and cook until 1 minute after the water returns to the boil. Scoop out the cabbage with a slotted spoon. Drain well. Reserve the cooking water.

5. Remove the sausages to a cutting board, leaving the sauce in the pan. Add the cabbage to the sauce; cook 15 minutes. Slice the sausage thin.

6. Return the water to a boil and cook the pasta with salt to taste. Drain well and toss with the sausage and the sauce. Serve hot.

Orecchiette with Swordfish

Orecchiette con Pesce Spada

Makes 4 to 6 servings

Tuna or shark can be substituted for the swordfish, if you prefer. Salting the eggplant removes some of the bitter juices and improves the texture, though many cooks feel this step is unnecessary. I always salt it, but the choice is up to you. The eggplant can be cooked several hours before the pasta. Simply reheat it on a baking sheet in a 350°F oven for 10 minutes or so before serving. This Sicilian pasta is unusual in Italian cooking in that even though the sauce contains fish, it is finished with cheese, adding to the richness.

1 large or 2 small eggplants (about 1½ pounds)

Coarse salt

Corn or other vegetable oil for frying

3 tablespoons olive oil

1 large garlic clove, very finely chopped

2 green onions, finely chopped

8 ounces swordfish or other meaty fish steak (about ½ inch thick), skin removed and cut into ½-inch pieces

Freshly ground black pepper to taste

2 tablespoons white wine vinegar

2 cups peeled, seeded, and chopped fresh tomatoes or chopped canned imported Italian tomatoes with their juice

1 teaspoon fresh oregano leaves, chopped, or a pinch of dried oregano

1 pound fresh orecchiette or cavatelli

⅓ cup freshly grated Pecorino Romano

1. Cut the eggplant into 1-inch dice. Place the pieces in a colander set over a plate and sprinkle generously with salt. Let stand 30 minutes to 1 hour. Quickly rinse the eggplant pieces. Place the pieces on paper towels and squeeze until dry.

2. In a large deep skillet over medium heat, heat about ½ inch of oil. To test the oil, carefully place a small piece of eggplant in it. If it sizzles and cooks rapidly, add enough eggplant to make a single layer. Do not crowd the pan. Cook, stirring occasionally, until the eggplant is crisp and browned, about 5 minutes.

Remove the pieces with a slotted spoon. Drain well on paper towels. Repeat with the remaining eggplant. Set aside.

3. In a medium skillet over medium heat, cook the olive oil with the garlic and green onions for 30 seconds. Add the fish and sprinkle with salt and pepper. Cook, stirring occasionally, until the fish is no longer pink, about 5 minutes. Add the vinegar and cook for 1 minute. Add the tomatoes and oregano. Bring to a simmer and cook for 15 minutes, or until slightly thickened.

4. Meanwhile, bring a large pot of cold water to a boil. Add salt to taste and the pasta. Cook, stirring occasionally, until al dente, tender yet firm to the bite. Drain well.

5. In a large heated serving bowl, combine the pasta, sauce, and eggplant. Toss well. Stir in the cheese. Serve hot.

Rice, Cornmeal, and Other Grains

Among the many types of grains grown and used throughout Italy, rice and cornmeal are the most common. Farro, couscous, and barley are regional favorites, as are wheat berries.

Rice was first brought to Italy from the Middle East. It grows particularly well in northern Italy, especially in the regions of Piedmont and Emilia-Romagna.

Italian cooks are very specific about the type of medium-grain rice they prefer, though the differences between varieties can be subtle. Many cooks will specify one variety for a seafood risotto and another for a risotto made with vegetables. Often, the preferences are regional or simply traditional, though each variety has specific properties. Carnaroli rice holds its shape well and makes a risotto that is slightly more creamy. Vialone Nano cooks faster and has a milder flavor. Arborio is the best known and is widely available, but the flavor is less subtle. It is best for risotto made with strong flavoring ingredients. Any of these three varieties can be used for the risotto recipes in this book.

Corn is a relatively new grain in Italy. It was not until after European exploration of the New World that corn found its way to

Spain and spread from there throughout the continent. Corn is easy and inexpensive to grow, so it quickly became widely planted. Most of it is grown for animal feed, but cornmeal, both white and yellow, is typically used for polenta. It is rare to find corn on the cob eaten in Italy, except in Naples, where vendors sometimes sell grilled corn as street food. Romans do sometimes add corn niblets from a can to tossed salads, but it is something of an exotic oddity.

Farro and similar wheatlike grains are most common in central and southern Italy where they are grown. An ancient variety of wheat, farro is regarded as a health food by Italians. It is excellent in soups, salads, and other preparations.

Barley is an ancient grain that grows well in the colder regions of the north. The Romans fed barley and other grains to their armies. It was cooked into a porridge or soup known as *puls*, probably the forerunner of polenta. Today you find barley mostly in the northeast of Italy, near Austria, cooked like risotto or added to soup.

Couscous, made from hard wheat flour rolled into tiny pellets, is typical in western Sicily and is a vestige of the Arab domination of the region centuries ago. It is usually cooked with a soupy seafood or meat stew.

RICE

Rice is grown in northern Italy in the Piedmont and Emilia-Romagna regions, and it is a staple that is often eaten in place of pasta or soup as a first course. The classic method for cooking rice is as risotto, which is my idea of rice in heaven!

If you have never made it before, the risotto technique may seem unusual. No other culture prepares rice in quite the same way as the Italians do, though the technique is similar to making pilaf, where the rice is sautéed and then cooked, and the cooking liquid absorbed. The idea is to cook the rice so that it releases its starch and forms a creamy sauce. The finished rice should be tender, yet still firm to the bite—al dente. The grains will have absorbed the flavors of the other ingredients and be surrounded by a creamy liquid. For best results, risotto needs to be eaten immediately after it is cooked or it may become dry and mushy.

Risotto is at its best when cooked at home. Few restaurants can devote as much time to the cooking of risotto as is needed, though it really isn't very long. In fact, many restaurant kitchens partially precook the rice, then cool it. When someone orders risotto, the rice is reheated, and liquid is added with whatever flavoring ingredients are needed to finish the cooking.

Once you understand the procedure, making risotto is quite simple and can be adapted to many different ingredient combinations. The first step in making risotto is getting the right type of rice. Long-grain rice, such as we commonly find in the United States, is not suitable for making risotto because it does not have the right kind of starch. Medium-grain rice, usually sold as Arborio, Carnaroli, or Vialone Nano varieties, has a kind of starch that releases from the grains when cooked and stirred with broth or another liquid. The starch binds with the liquid and becomes creamy.

Medium-grain rice imported from Italy is widely available in supermarkets. It is also grown in the United States and is now easy to find.

You will also need good chicken, meat, fish, or vegetable broth. Homemade is preferable, but canned (or boxed) broth can be used. I find store-bought broth too strong to use straight out of the container and often dilute it with water. Remember that packaged broth, unless you use a low-sodium variety, contains a lot of salt, so adjust any added salt accordingly. Boullion cubes are very salty and artificial-tasting, so I do not use them.

White Risotto

Risotto in Bianco

Makes 4 servings

This plain white risotto is as basic and satisfying as vanilla ice cream. Serve it as is as a first course or as a side dish with braised meats. If you happen to have a fresh truffle, try shaving it over the finished risotto for a luxurious touch. In that case, you should eliminate the cheese.

    4 cups Meat Broth or Chicken Broth

4 tablespoons unsalted butter

1 tablespoon olive oil

¼ cup minced shallots or onion

1½ cups medium-grain rice, such as Arborio, Carnaroli, or Vialone Nano

½ cup dry white wine or sparkling wine

Salt and freshly ground black pepper

½ cup freshly grated Parmigiano-Reggiano

1. Prepare the broth, if necessary. Bring the broth to a simmer over medium heat, then lower the heat so that it is just keeping the broth hot. In a wide heavy saucepan, melt 3 tablespoons of the butter with the oil over medium heat. Add the shallots and cook until softened but not browned, about 5 minutes.

2. Add the rice and stir with a wooden spoon until hot, about 2 minutes. Add the wine and cook, stirring, until most of the liquid evaporates.

3. Pour $1/2$ cup of the broth over the rice. Cook, stirring, until most of the liquid is absorbed. Continue adding broth about $1/2$ cup at a time, stirring after each addition. Adjust the heat so that the liquid simmers rapidly but the rice does not stick to the pan. About halfway through the cooking time, add salt and pepper to taste.

4. Use only as much of the broth as needed until the rice becomes tender yet firm to the bite and the risotto is creamy. When you think it may be done, taste a few grains. If not ready, test again in a minute or so. If the broth runs out before the rice is tender, use hot water. Cooking time will be 18 to 20 minutes.

5. Remove the risotto pan from the heat. Stir in the remaining tablespoon of butter and cheese until melted and creamy. Serve immediately.

Saffron Risotto, Milan Style

Risotto Milanese

Makes 4 to 6 servings

Golden risotto flavored with saffron is the classic Milanese accompaniment to Osso Buco (see <u>Veal Shanks, Milan Style</u>). Adding marrow scooped out of large beef bones to the risotto lends a rich, beefy flavor and is traditional, but the risotto can be made without it.

6 cups <u>Chicken Broth</u> or <u>Meat Broth</u>

½ teaspoon crumbled saffron threads

4 tablespoons unsalted butter

2 tablespoons beef marrow (optional)

2 tablespoons olive oil

1 small onion, very finely chopped

2 cups (about 1 pound) medium-grain rice, such as Arborio, Carnaroli, or Vialone Nano

Salt and freshly ground black pepper

½ cup freshly grated Parmigiano-Reggiano

1. Prepare the broth, if necessary. Bring the broth to a simmer over medium heat, then lower the heat so it is just keeping the broth hot. Remove ½ cup broth and put in a small bowl. Add the saffron and allow it to soak.

2. In a wide heavy saucepan, heat 2 tablespoons of the butter, the marrow if using, and the oil over medium heat. When the butter is melted, add the onion and cook, stirring often, until golden, about 10 minutes.

3. Add the rice and cook, stirring with a wooden spoon until hot, about 2 minutes. Add ½ cup of the hot broth and stir until the liquid is absorbed. Continue adding the broth ½ cup at a time, stirring after each addition. Adjust the heat so that the liquid simmers rapidly but the rice does not stick to the pan. About halfway through the cooking time, stir in the saffron mixture and salt and pepper to taste.

4. Use only as much of the broth as needed until the rice becomes tender yet firm to the bite. When you think it may be done, taste a few grains. If not ready, test again in a minute or so. If the broth runs out before the rice is tender, use hot water. Cooking time will be 18 to 20 minutes.

5. Remove the risotto pan from the heat and stir in the remaining 2 tablespoons of butter and the cheese until melted and creamy. Serve immediately.

Asparagus Risotto

Risotto con Asparagi

Makes 6 servings

The Veneto region is famous for its beautiful lavender-tipped white asparagus. To achieve the delicate color, the asparagus are kept covered as they grow so that they are not exposed to sunlight and do not form chlorophyll. White asparagus have a delicate flavor and are more tender than the green variety. White asparagus is ideal for this risotto, but you can make it with the ordinary green variety and the flavor will still be very good.

5 cups <u>Chicken Broth</u>

1 pound fresh asparagus, trimmed

4 tablespoons unsalted butter

1 small onion, finely chopped

2 cups medium-grain rice, such as Arborio, Carnaroli, or Vialone Nano

½ cup dry white wine

Salt and freshly ground black pepper

¾ cup freshly grated Parmigiano-Reggiano

1. Prepare the broth, if necessary. Bring the broth to a simmer over medium heat, then lower the heat so that it just keeps the broth hot. Cut off the asparagus tips and set them aside. Cut the stems into $1/2$-inch slices.

2. Melt 3 tablespoons of the butter in a wide, heavy saucepan. Add the onion and cook over medium heat, stirring occasionally, until very tender and golden, about 10 minutes.

3. Stir in the asparagus stems. Cook, stirring occasionally, 5 minutes.

4. Add the rice and cook, stirring with a wooden spoon until hot, about 2 minutes. Add the wine and cook, stirring constantly, until the liquid evaporates. Pour $1/2$ cup of the broth over the rice. Cook, stirring, until most of the liquid is absorbed.

5. Continue adding broth about $1/2$ cup at a time, stirring after each addition. Adjust the heat so that the liquid simmers rapidly but the rice does not stick to the pan. After about 10 minutes, stir in the asparagus tips. Season with salt and pepper. Use only as much of the broth as needed until the rice becomes tender yet firm to the bite and the risotto is creamy. When you think it may be done, taste a few grains. If not ready, test again in a minute or

so. If the broth runs out before the rice is tender, use hot water. Cooking time will be 18 to 20 minutes.

6. Remove the risotto pan from the heat. Stir in the cheese and the remaining tablespoon butter. Taste for seasoning. Serve immediately.

Risotto with Red Peppers

Risotto con Peperoni Rossi

Makes 6 servings

At the height of the season when brilliant red bell peppers are piled high at the greengrocers, I am inspired to use them in many ways. Their sweet, mellow flavor and gorgeous color make everything from omelets to pastas, soups, salads, and stews taste better. This is not a traditional recipe, but one I came up with one day while looking for a new way to use some red peppers. Yellow or orange peppers would be good in this recipe, too.

   5 cups <u>Chicken Broth</u>

3 tablespoons unsalted butter

1 tablespoon olive oil

1 small onion, finely chopped

2 red bell peppers, seeded and finely chopped

2 cups medium-grain rice, such as Arborio, Carnaroli, or Vialone Nano

Salt and freshly ground black pepper

½ cup freshly grated Parmigiano-Reggiano

1. Prepare the broth, if necessary. Bring the broth to a simmer over medium heat, then lower the heat so that it just keeps the broth hot. In a wide heavy saucepan, heat 2 tablespoons of the butter and the oil over medium heat. When the butter is melted, add the onion and cook, stirring often until golden, about 10 minutes. Add the peppers and cook 10 minutes more.

2. Add the rice and stir with a wooden spoon until hot, about 2 minutes. Add ½ cup of the hot broth and stir until the liquid is absorbed. Continue adding the broth a ½ cup at a time, stirring after each addition. Adjust the heat so that the liquid simmers rapidly but the rice does not stick to the pan. About halfway through the cooking, add salt and pepper to taste.

3. Use only as much of the broth as needed until the rice becomes tender yet firm to the bite and the risotto is creamy. When you think it may be done, taste a few grains. If not ready, test again in a minute or so. If the liquid runs out before the rice is cooked, finish the cooking with hot water. Cooking time will be 18 to 20 minutes.

4. Remove the risotto pan from the heat. Stir in the remaining tablespoon of butter and the cheese until melted and creamy. Taste for seasoning. Serve immediately.

Tomato and Arugula Risotto

Risotto con Pomodori e Rucola

Makes 6 servings

Fresh tomatoes, basil, and arugula make this risotto the essence of summer. I love to serve it with a cool white wine, such as Campania's Furore from producer Matilde Cuomo.

- 5 cups <u>Chicken Broth</u>
- 1 large bunch arugula, trimmed and rinsed
- 3 tablespoons olive oil
- 1 small onion, finely chopped
- 2 pounds ripe plum tomatoes, peeled, seeded, and chopped
- 2 cups medium-grain rice, such as Arborio, Carnaroli, or Vialone Nano
- Salt and freshly ground black pepper
- ½ cup freshly grated Parmigiano-Reggiano
- 2 tablespoons chopped fresh basil
- 1 tablespoon extra-virgin olive oil

1. Prepare the broth, if necessary. Bring the broth to a simmer over medium heat, then lower the heat so that it just keeps the broth hot. Tear the arugula leaves into bite size pieces. You should have about 2 cups.

2. Pour the oil into a wide heavy saucepan. Add the onion and cook over medium heat, stirring occasionally with a wooden spoon, until the onion is very tender and golden, about 10 minutes.

3. Stir in the tomatoes. Cook, stirring occasionally, until most of the juice has evaporated, about 10 minutes.

4. Add the rice and cook, stirring with a wooden spoon until hot, about 2 minutes. Pour $1/2$ cup of the broth over the rice. Cook and stir until most of the liquid is absorbed.

5. Continue adding broth about $1/2$ cup at a time, stirring after each addition. Adjust the heat so that the liquid simmers rapidly but the rice does not stick to the pan. Halfway through the cooking, season with salt and pepper. Use only as much of the broth as needed until the rice becomes tender yet firm to the bite and the risotto is creamy. When you think it may be done, taste a few grains. If not ready, test again in a minute or so. If the broth runs out before the rice is tender, use hot water. Cooking time will be 18 to 20 minutes.

6. Remove the risotto pan from the heat. Stir in the cheese, basil, and a tablespoon of extra-virgin olive oil. Taste for seasoning. Stir in the arugula and serve immediately.

Risotto with Red Wine and Radicchio

Risotto al Radicchio

Makes 6 servings

Radicchio, a member of the chicory family, is grown in the Veneto. Like endive, to which it is related, radicchio has a slightly bitter-yet-sweet flavor. Though we think of it mostly as a colorful addition to a salad bowl, the Italians often cook radicchio. It can be cut into wedges and grilled, or the leaves can be wrapped around a filling and baked as an appetizer. The vibrant wine-red color turns a dark mahogany brown when it is cooked. I had this risotto at Il Cenacolo, a restaurant in Verona that features traditional recipes.

    5 cups Chicken Broth or Meat Broth

1 medium head radicchio (about 12 ounces)

2 tablespoons olive oil

2 tablespoons unsalted butter

1 small onion, finely chopped

½ cup dry red wine

2 cups medium-grain rice, such as Arborio, Carnaroli, or Vialone Nano

Salt and freshly ground black pepper

½ cup freshly grated Parmigiano-Reggiano

1. Prepare the broth, if necessary. Bring the broth to a simmer over medium heat, then lower the heat so that it just keeps the broth hot. Trim the radicchio and cut it into ½-inch-thick slices. Cut the slices into 1 inch lengths.

2. In a wide heavy saucepan, heat the oil with 1 tablespoon of the butter over medium heat. When the butter is melted, add the onion and cook, stirring occasionally, until the onion is very tender, about 10 minutes.

3. Raise the heat to medium, stir in the radicchio, and cook until wilted, about 10 minutes.

4. Stir in the rice. Add the wine and cook, stirring, until most of the liquid is absorbed. Pour ½ cup of the broth over the rice. Cook and stir until most of the liquid is absorbed.

5. Continue adding broth about ½ cup at a time, stirring after each addition. Adjust the heat so that the liquid simmers rapidly but the rice does not stick to the pan. Halfway through the cooking, season with salt and pepper. Use only as much of the broth as needed until the rice becomes tender yet firm to the

bite and the risotto is creamy. When you think it may be done, taste a few grains. If not ready, test again in a minute or so. If the broth runs out before the rice is tender, use hot water. Cooking time will be 18 to 20 minutes.

6. Remove the saucepan from the heat and stir in the remaining tablespoon of butter and the cheese. Taste for seasoning. Serve immediately.

Risotto with Creamy Cauliflower

Risotto al Cavolfiore

Makes 6 servings

In Parma, you might not eat an appetizer or a main course, but you would never want to miss an opportunity to have risotto or pasta; they are always incredibly good. This is my version of a risotto I had there some years ago at La Filoma, an excellent trattoria.

The first time I made this risotto, I happened to have a tube of white truffle paste on hand, and I stirred some in at the end of the cooking time. The flavor was sensational. Try it if you can find truffle paste.

    4 cups Chicken Broth

4 cups cauliflower, chopped into ½-inch florets

1 garlic clove, finely chopped

1½ cups milk

Salt

4 tablespoons unsalted butter

¼ cup finely chopped onion

2 cups medium-grain rice, such as Arborio, Carnaroli, or Vialone Nano

Freshly ground black pepper

¾ cup freshly grated Parmigiano-Reggiano

1. Prepare the broth, if necessary. Bring the broth to a simmer over medium heat, then lower the heat so that it just keeps the broth hot. In a medium saucepan, combine the cauliflower, garlic, milk, and a pinch of salt. Bring to a simmer. Cook until most of the liquid is evaporated and the cauliflower is soft, about 10 minutes. Keep the heat very low and stir the mixture occasionally so that it does not scorch.

2. In a wide heavy saucepan, heat the oil with 2 tablespoons of the butter over medium heat. When the butter is melted, add the onion and cook, stirring occasionally, until the onion is very tender and golden, about 10 minutes.

3. Add the rice and cook, stirring with a wooden spoon until hot, about 2 minutes. Pour in about ½ cup of the broth. Cook and stir until most of the liquid is absorbed.

4. Continue adding the broth ½ cup at a time, stirring constantly, until it is absorbed. Adjust the heat so that the liquid simmers

rapidly but the rice does not stick to the pan. About halfway through the cooking, season with salt and pepper.

5. When the rice is almost done, stir in the cauliflower mixture. Use only as much of the broth as needed until the rice becomes tender yet firm to the bite and the risotto is creamy. When you think it may be done, taste a few grains. If not ready, test again in a minute or so. If the broth runs out before the rice is tender, use hot water. Cooking time will be 18 to 20 minutes.

6. Remove the saucepan from the heat and taste for seasoning. Stir in the remaining 2 tablespoons of butter and the cheese. Serve immediately.

Lemon Risotto

Risotto al Limone

Makes 6 servings

The lively flavor of fresh lemon zest and juice brightens up this risotto that I ate in Capri. Though the Italians don't often do it, I like to serve it as a side dish with sautéed scallops or grilled fish.

   5 cups <u>Chicken Broth</u>

4 tablespoons unsalted butter

1 small onion, finely chopped

2 cups medium-grain rice, such as Arborio, Carnaroli, or Vialone Nano

Salt and freshly ground black pepper

1 tablespoon fresh lemon juice

1 teaspoon grated lemon zest

½ cup freshly grated Parmigiano-Reggiano

1. Prepare the broth, if necessary. Bring the broth to a simmer over medium heat, then lower the heat so that it just keeps the broth hot. In a wide heavy saucepan, melt 2 tablespoons of the butter over medium heat. Add the onion and cook, stirring often until golden, about 10 minutes.

2. Add the rice and stir with a wooden spoon until hot, about 2 minutes. Add $1/2$ cup of the hot broth and stir until the liquid is absorbed.

3. Continue adding the broth $1/2$ cup at a time, stirring after each addition. Adjust the heat so that the liquid simmers rapidly but the rice does not stick to the pan. About halfway through the cooking time, season with salt and pepper.

4. Use only as much of the broth as needed until the rice becomes tender yet firm to the bite and the risotto is creamy. When you think it may be done, taste a few grains. If not ready, test again in a minute or so. If the broth runs out before the rice is tender, use hot water. Cooking time will be 18 to 20 minutes.

5. Remove the risotto pan from the heat. Add the lemon juice and zest, the remaining 2 tablespoons of butter, and the cheese. Stir until the butter and cheese are melted and creamy. Taste for seasoning. Serve immediately.

Spinach Risotto

Risotto agli Spinaci

Makes 6 servings

If you have some fresh basil, add that instead of the parsley. Other greens such as Swiss chard or escarole can be used in place of spinach.

5 cups Chicken Broth

1 pound fresh spinach, washed and stems removed

¼ cup water

Salt

4 tablespoons unsalted butter

1 medium onion, finely chopped

2 cups (about 1 pound) medium-grain rice, such as Arborio, Carnaroli, or Vialone Nano

Freshly ground black pepper

¼ cup chopped fresh flat-leaf parsley

½ cup freshly grated Parmigiano-Reggiano

1. Prepare the broth, if necessary. Bring the broth to a simmer over medium heat, then lower the heat so that it just keeps the broth hot. In a large pot, combine the spinach, water, and salt to taste. Cover and bring to a simmer. Cook until the spinach is wilted, about 3 minutes. Drain the spinach and squeeze lightly to extract the juices. Finely chop the spinach.

2. In a wide heavy saucepan, heat 3 tablespoons of the butter over medium heat. When the butter is melted, add the onion and cook, stirring often, until golden, about 10 minutes

3. Add the rice to the onion and cook, stirring with a wooden spoon, until hot, about 2 minutes. Add ½ cup of the hot broth and stir until the liquid is absorbed. Continue adding the broth ½ cup at a time, stirring after each addition. Adjust the heat so that the liquid simmers rapidly but the rice does not stick to the pan. Halfway through the cooking, stir in the spinach and salt and pepper to taste.

4. Use only as much of the broth as needed until the rice becomes tender yet firm to the bite and the risotto is creamy. When you think it may be done, taste a few grains. If not ready, test again in

a minute or so. If the broth runs out before the rice is tender, use hot water. Cooking time will be 18 to 20 minutes.

5. Remove the risotto pan from the heat. Stir in the remaining butter and the cheese. Serve immediately.

Golden Squash Risotto

Risotto con Zucca d'Oro

Makes 4 to 6 servings

In Italian greenmarkets, cooks can buy wedges of large winter squash to use for risotto. Butternut squash comes closest to the sweet flavor and buttery texture of the Italian varieties. This risotto is a specialty of Mantua in Lombardy.

> 5 cups Chicken Broth

4 tablespoons unsalted butter

¼ cup finely chopped shallots or onion

2 cups peeled and chopped butternut squash (about 1 pound)

2 cups medium-grain rice, such as Arborio, Carnaroli, or Vialone Nano

½ cup dry white wine

Salt and freshly ground black pepper

½ cup freshly grated Parmigiano-Reggiano

1. Prepare the broth, if necessary. Bring the broth to a simmer over medium heat, then lower the heat so that it just keeps the broth hot. In a wide heavy saucepan, melt three tablespoons of the butter over medium heat. Add the shallots and cook, stirring often until golden, about 5 minutes.

2. Add the squash and $1/2$ cup of the broth. Cook until the broth evaporates.

3. Add the rice and cook, stirring with a wooden spoon until hot, about 2 minutes. Stir in the wine until it evaporates.

4. Add $1/2$ cup of the hot broth and stir until the liquid is absorbed. Continue adding the broth $1/2$ cup at a time, stirring after each addition. Adjust the heat so that the liquid simmers rapidly but the rice does not stick to the pan. Halfway through the cooking, stir in salt and pepper to taste.

5. Use only as much of the broth as needed until the rice becomes tender yet firm to the bite and the risotto is creamy. When you think it may be done, taste a few grains. If not ready, test again in a minute or so. If the broth runs out before the rice is tender, use hot water. Cooking time will be 18 to 20 minutes.

6. Remove the risotto pan from the heat. Stir in the remaining butter and the cheese. Serve immediately.

Venetian Risotto with Peas

Risi e Bisi

Makes 6 servings

In Venice, this risotto is eaten to celebrate the coming of spring and the first of the season's fresh vegetables. Venetians prefer their risotto rather soupy, so add an extra spoonful or so of broth or water to the finished risotto if you're going for authenticity.

6 cups <u>Chicken Broth</u>

1 medium yellow onion, finely chopped

4 tablespoons olive oil

2 cups medium-grain rice, such as Arborio, Carnaroli, or Vialone Nano

Salt and freshly ground black pepper

2 cups shelled tender peas, or frozen peas, partially thawed

2 tablespoons finely chopped flat-leaf parsley

½ cup freshly grated Parmigiano-Reggiano

2 tablespoons unsalted butter

1. Prepare the broth, if necessary. Bring the broth to a simmer over medium heat, then lower the heat so that it just keeps the broth hot. Pour the oil into a wide heavy saucepan. Add the onion and cook over medium heat until the onion is tender and golden, about 10 minutes.

2. Add the rice and cook, stirring with a wooden spoon, until hot, about 2 minutes. Add about $1/2$ cup of the hot broth and stir until it is absorbed. Continue adding broth $1/2$ cup at a time, stirring after each addition. Adjust the heat so that the liquid simmers rapidly but the rice does not stick to the pan. Halfway through the cooking, stir in salt and pepper to taste.

3. Add the peas and parsley. Continue adding the liquid and stirring. The rice should be tender yet firm to the bite, and the risotto should have a loose, somewhat soupy, consistency. Use hot water if you run out of broth. Cooking time will be 18 to 20 minutes.

4. When the rice is tender yet still firm, remove the pot from the heat. Add the cheese and butter and stir well. Serve immediately.

Springtime Risotto

Risotto Primavera

Makes 4 to 6 servings

Tiny pieces of colorful vegetables spangle this bright and flavorful risotto. The vegetables are added in stages so that they do not overcook.

6 cups vegetable broth or water

3 tablespoons unsalted butter

1 tablespoon olive oil

1 medium onion, finely chopped

1 small carrot, chopped

1 small tender celery rib, chopped

2 cups medium-grain rice, such as Arborio, Carnaroli, or Vialone Nano

1/2 cup fresh or frozen peas

1 cup sliced mushrooms, any kind

6 asparagus, trimmed and cut into 1/2-inch pieces

Salt and freshly ground black pepper

1 large tomato, seeded and diced

2 tablespoons finely chopped fresh flat-leaf parsley

½ cup freshly grated Parmigiano-Reggiano

1. Prepare the broth, if necessary. Bring the broth to a simmer over medium heat, then lower the heat so that it just keeps the broth hot. In a wide heavy saucepan, combine 2 tablespoons of the butter and the oil over medium heat. When the butter has melted, add the onion and cook until it turns golden, about 10 minutes.

2. Add the carrot and celery and cook 2 minutes. Stir in the rice until well coated.

3. Add ½ cup of the broth and cook, stirring constantly with a wooden spoon, until the liquid is absorbed. Continue adding broth ½ cup at a time, stirring after each addition, for 10 minutes. Adjust the heat so that the liquid simmers rapidly but the rice does not stick to the pan.

4. Stir in the peas, mushrooms, and half of the asparagus. Add salt and pepper to taste. Continue adding broth and stirring 10 minutes more. Stir in the remaining asparagus and tomato. Add

broth and stir until the rice is firm yet tender to the bite and the risotto is creamy. When you think it may be done, taste a few grains. If not ready, test again in a minute or so.

5. Remove the risotto pan from the heat. Taste for seasoning. Stir in the parsley and remaining butter. Stir in the cheese. Serve immediately.

Risotto with Tomatoes and Fontina

Risotto con Pomodori e Fontina

Makes 6 servings

Genuine Fontina Valle d'Aosta has a pronounced flavor that is nutty, fruity, and earthy, unlike fontina made elsewhere. It is worth seeking out for this risotto from northwestern Italy. This dish would go well with a floral white wine such as Arneis, from the nearby Piedmont region.

5 cups [Chicken Broth](#)

3 tablespoons unsalted butter

1 medium onion, finely chopped

1 cup peeled, seeded, and chopped tomatoes

2 cups medium-grain rice, such as Arborio, Carnaroli, or Vialone Nano

½ cup dry white wine

Salt and freshly ground black pepper

4 ounces Fontina Valle d'Aosta, shredded

½ cup freshly grated Parmigiano-Reggiano

1. Prepare the broth, if necessary. Bring the broth to a simmer over medium heat, then lower the heat so that it just keeps the broth hot. Melt the butter in a wide heavy saucepan over medium heat. Add the onion and cook, stirring occasionally, until the onion is tender and golden, about 10 minutes.

2. Stir in the tomatoes. Cook until most of the liquid has evaporated, about 10 minutes.

3. Add the rice and cook, stirring with a wooden spoon, until hot, about 2 minutes. Pour the wine and $1/2$ cup of the broth over the rice. Cook and stir until most of the liquid is absorbed.

4. Continue adding broth about $1/2$ cup at a time, stirring after each addition. Adjust the heat so that the liquid simmers rapidly but the rice does not stick to the pan. About halfway through the cooking, season with salt and pepper to taste.

5. Use only as much of the broth as needed until the rice becomes tender yet firm to the bite and the risotto is creamy. When you think it may be done, taste a few grains. If not ready, test again in a minute or so. If the broth runs out before the rice is tender, use hot water. Cooking time is 18 to 20 minutes.

6. Remove the risotto pan from the heat. Stir in the cheeses. Taste for seasoning. Serve immediately.

Shrimp and Celery Risotto

Risotto con Gamberi e Sedano

Makes 6 servings

Many Italian recipes are flavored with a soffritto, *a combination of either oil or butter, or sometimes both, and aromatic vegetables, which can include but are not limited to onion, celery, carrot, garlic, and sometimes herbs. Sometimes salt pork or pancetta is added to a soffritto for a meaty flavor.*

Like most of the Italian cooks I know, I prefer to put the soffritto ingredients into the pot all at once, then turn on the heat so that everything warms up and cooks gently and I can control the results better. I stir the soffritto often, sometimes cooking until the vegetables are just wilted for a mild flavor, or until they are golden brown for greater depth. If, instead, you heat the oil or butter first, the fat can become too hot if the pan is thin, the heat is a little too high, or you are momentarily distracted. Then when the other soffritto flavorings are added, they brown too rapidly and unevenly.

The soffritto for this recipe from Emilia-Romagna is made in two stages. It begins with only the olive oil and onion, because I want the onion to release its flavor to the oil and fade somewhat into the background. The second stage is cooking the celery, parsley, and garlic so that the celery remains a little crunchy and yet releases its flavor and creates another taste layer with the parsley and garlic.

If you buy shrimp with their shells on, save the shells to make a tasty shrimp broth. If you are in a hurry, you can buy shelled shrimp and just use the chicken or fish broth, or even water.

6 cups homemade <u>Chicken Broth</u> or store-bought fish stock

1 pound medium shrimp

1 small onion, finely chopped

2 tablespoons olive oil

1 cup finely chopped celery

2 garlic cloves, finely chopped

2 tablespoons chopped fresh flat-leaf parsley

2 cups medium-grain rice, such as Arborio, Carnaroli, or Vialone Nano

Salt and freshly ground black pepper to taste

1 tablespoon unsalted butter or extra-virgin olive oil

1. Prepare the broth, if necessary. Then, shell and devein the shrimp, reserving the shells. Cut the shrimp into $1/2$-inch pieces and set aside. Place the shells in a large saucepan with the broth. Bring to a simmer and cook 10 minutes. Strain the broth and discard the shells. Return the broth to the pan and keep over very low heat.

2. In a wide heavy saucepan, cook the onion in the oil over medium heat, stirring frequently, about 5 minutes. Stir in the celery, garlic, and parsley and cook 5 minutes more.

3. Add the rice to the vegetables and stir thoroughly to combine. Add $1/2$ cup of the broth and cook, stirring, until the liquid is absorbed. Continue adding the broth $1/2$ cup at a time, stirring after each addition. Adjust the heat so that the liquid simmers rapidly but the rice does not stick to the pan.

4. When the rice is almost done, stir in the shrimp and salt and pepper to taste. Use only as much of the broth as needed until the rice becomes tender yet firm to the bite and the risotto is moist and creamy. When you think it may be done, taste a few grains. If not ready, test again in a minute or so. If the broth runs out before the rice is tender, use hot water. Cooking time is 18 to 20 minutes.

5. Remove the risotto from the heat. Add the butter or oil and stir until blended. Serve immediately.

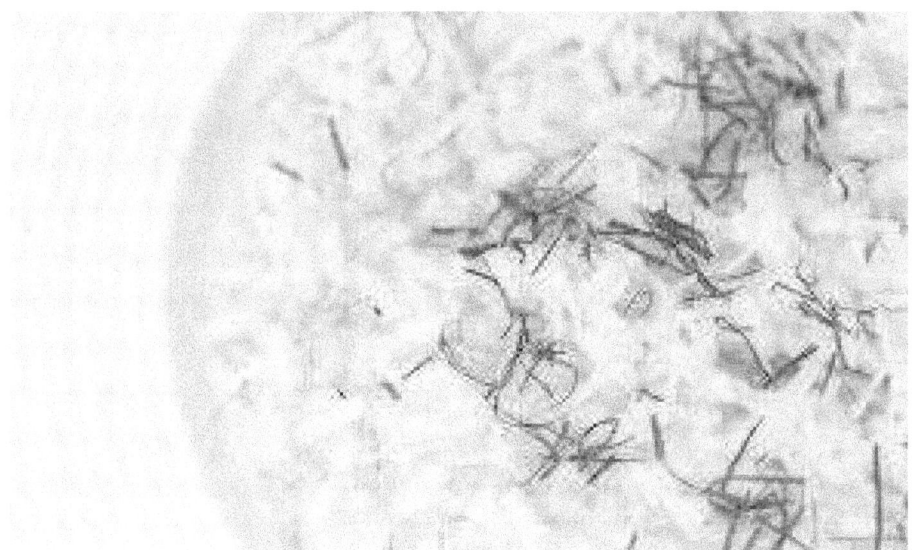

Risotto with "Fruits of the Sea"

Risotto con Frutti di Mare

Makes 4 to 6 servings

Tiny clams or mussels can be added to this risotto, or even bits of firm fish such as tuna. Cooks in the Veneto, where this recipe originated, prefer the Vialone Nano variety of rice.

6 cups Chicken Broth or water

6 tablespoons olive oil

2 tablespoons chopped fresh flat-leaf parsley

2 large garlic cloves, finely chopped

½ pound calamari (squid), cut into ½-inch rings and tentacles halved through the base (see Cleaning Calamari (Squid))

¼ pound shrimp, shelled and deveined and cut into ½-inch pieces

¼ pound scallops, cut into ½-inch pieces

Salt

Pinch of crushed red pepper

1 medium onion, finely chopped

2 cups medium-grain rice, such as Arborio, Carnaroli, or Vialone Nano

½ cup dry white wine

1 cup peeled, seeded, and chopped tomatoes

1. Prepare the broth, if necessary. Put 3 tablespoons oil with the garlic and parsley into a wide heavy saucepan. Cook over medium heat, stirring occasionally, until the garlic is softened and golden, about 2 minutes. Add all the seafood, salt to taste, and red pepper and cook, stirring until the calamari are just opaque, about 5 minutes.

2. With a slotted spoon, remove the seafood to a plate. Add the chicken broth to the pan and bring to a simmer. Keep the broth over very low heat while cooking the risotto.

3. In a wide heavy saucepan, over medium heat, cook the onion in the remaining 3 tablespoons of the oil until golden, about 10 minutes.

4. Add the rice and cook, stirring with a wooden spoon, until hot, about 2 minutes. Stir in the wine. Cook until most of the liquid is absorbed. Add ½ cup of the hot broth and stir until the liquid is absorbed. Continue adding the broth ½ cup at a time, stirring after each addition. Adjust the heat so that the liquid simmers rapidly but the rice does not stick to the pan. About halfway through the cooking, stir in the tomato, and salt to taste.

5. Use only as much of the broth as needed until the rice becomes tender yet firm to the bite and the risotto is creamy. When you think it may be done, taste a few grains. If not ready, test again in a minute or so. If the broth runs out before the rice is tender, use hot water. Cooking time is 18 to 20 minutes.

6. Add the seafood to the pot and cook 1 minute more. Remove the risotto pan from the heat. Serve immediately.

"Sea and Mountain" Risotto

Risotto Maremonti

Makes 6 servings

When you see the term maremonti *on a menu in Italy, you can be sure the dish will contain seafood and mushrooms, representing the sea and the mountains. It is an intriguing combination in this risotto.*

6 cups store-bought vegetable broth or water

3 tablespoons unsalted butter

¼ cup finely chopped shallots

10 ounces cremini or white mushrooms, thinly sliced

Salt and freshly ground black pepper

2 cups medium-grain rice, such as Arborio, Carnaroli, or Vialone Nano

12 ounces shelled and deveined shrimp, cut into ½-inch pieces

½ cup freshly grated Parmigiano-Reggiano

1. In a large pot, bring the broth to a simmer over medium heat, then lower the heat so that it just keeps the broth hot. In a wide heavy saucepan, melt 2 tablespoons of the butter over medium heat. Add the shallots and mushrooms. Cook, stirring frequently, until the juices evaporate and the mushrooms begin to turn brown, about 10 minutes. Stir in salt and pepper to taste.

2. Add the rice and cook, stirring with a wooden spoon until hot, about 2 minutes. Add 1/2 cup of the hot broth and stir until the liquid is absorbed. Continue adding the broth 1/2 cup at a time, stirring after each addition. Adjust the heat so that the liquid simmers rapidly but the rice does not stick to the pan. About halfway through the cooking, stir in the shrimp and salt and pepper to taste.

3. Use only as much of the broth as needed until the rice becomes tender yet firm to the bite and the risotto is creamy. When you think it may be done, taste a few grains. If not ready, test again in a minute or so. If the broth runs out before the rice is tender, use hot water. Cooking time is 18 to 20 minutes.

4. Remove the risotto pan from the heat. Stir in the remaining 1 tablespoon butter. Stir in the cheese and serve immediately.

Black Risotto

Risotto alle Seppie

Makes 4 to 6 servings

In Venice, calamari (squid) or cuttlefish ink traditionally turns this risotto a caviar-like shade of black. Most seafood in the United States has the ink sac removed before you buy it, but you can purchase squid ink in small plastic envelopes at most seafood stores. The calamari and its ink are so flavorful that I make this risotto with water rather than broth so that there is nothing to interfere with their briny flavor.

6 cups water

4 tablespoons olive oil

1 medium onion, finely chopped

1 garlic clove, finely chopped

12 ounces calamari (squid), cut into $\frac{1}{2}$-inch rings and tentacles halved through the base (see Cleaning Calamari (Squid))

Salt and freshly ground black pepper

1 cup dry white wine

2 cups medium-grain rice, such as Arborio, Carnaroli, or Vialone Nano

1 to 2 teaspoons squid or cuttlefish ink (optional)

1 to 2 tablespoons extra-virgin olive oil

1. In a medium saucepan, bring the water to a simmer over medium heat, then lower the heat so that it just keeps the water hot.

2. Pour 4 tablespoons oil in a wide heavy saucepan. Add the onion and cook over medium heat, stirring frequently, until tender and golden, about 10 minutes. Add the calamari, and salt and pepper to taste. Cover the pan and cook 10 minutes. Add the wine and cook 1 minute more.

3. Add the rice and cook, stir with a wooden spoon, until hot, about 2 minutes. Add $1/2$ cup of the hot water and stir until the liquid is absorbed. Continue adding the water $1/2$ cup at a time, stirring after each addition. Adjust the heat so that the liquid simmers rapidly but the rice does not stick to the pan. Halfway through the cooking, stir in the squid ink, if using, and salt to taste.

4. Use only as much of the water as needed until the rice becomes tender yet firm to the bite and the risotto is creamy. When you

think it may be done, taste a few grains. If not ready, test again in a minute or so. Cooking time is 18 to 20 minutes.

5. Remove risotto pan from the heat. Stir in the oil until blended. Serve immediately.

Crisp Risotto Pancake

Risotto al Salto

Makes 2 to 4 servings

This golden risotto pancake is crisp on the outside and creamy on the inside. In Milan, the pancake is called risotto al salto, *meaning "jumping risotto," because it is cooked in hot butter, which makes it seem to jump out of the pan. Though the Milanese typically prepare the pancake with leftover* Saffron Risotto, Milan Style, *I use all kinds of risotto and sometimes make it from scratch just for this purpose.*

You can serve the pancake in many ways—plain, with a tomato sauce and sprinkled with cheese, or as the base for a stew. You can cut it into wedges to accompany a salad or to serve as an appetizer. You can also make tiny silver-dollar-size pancakes for individual appetizers or snacks.

2 cups cold leftover risotto

1 large egg, beaten

2 tablespoons unsalted butter

1. In a medium bowl, mix together the risotto and the egg until well blended.

2. In a medium nonstick skillet over medium heat, melt 1 tablespoon butter. Add the risotto and flatten it out with a spoon. Cook until crusty and golden brown on the bottom, about 5 minutes.

3. Flip the pancake onto a dinner plate. Melt the remaining butter and slide the pancake back into the pan. Flatten it well with the back of the spoon. Cook until golden, 4 to 5 minutes more.

4. Slide the pancake onto a plate. Cut into wedges and serve hot.

Butter Rings

Bussolai

Makes 36

These Venetian cookies are simple to make and a pleasure to have around the house for a midday snack or whenever guests stop in.

1 cup sugar

½ cup (1 stick) unsalted butter, at room temperature

3 large egg yolks

1 teaspoon grated lemon zest

1 teaspoon grated orange zest

1 teaspoon pure vanilla extract

2 cups all-purpose flour

½ teaspoon salt

1 egg white, beaten until foamy

1. Set aside $1/3$ cup of the sugar.

2. In the large bowl of an electric mixer, beat the butter with the remaining ⅔ cup of sugar at medium speed until light and fluffy, about 2 minutes. Beat in the egg yolks one at a time. Add the lemon and orange zests and vanilla extract and beat, scraping the sides of the bowl, until smooth, about 2 minutes more.

3. Stir in the flour and salt until well blended. Shape the dough into a ball. Wrap in plastic wrap and refrigerate 1 hour up to overnight.

4. Preheat the oven to 325°F. Grease 2 large baking sheets. Cut the dough into 6 pieces. Divide each piece again into 6 pieces. Roll each piece into a 4-inch rope, shape into a ring, and pinch the ends together to seal. Place the rings 1 inch apart on the prepared baking sheets. Brush lightly with the egg white and sprinkle with the reserved ⅓ cup of sugar.

5. Bake 15 minutes or until lightly browned. Have ready 2 wire cooling racks.

6. Transfer the baking sheets to the racks. Let the cookies cool 5 minutes on the baking sheets, then transfer them to the wire racks to cool completely. Store in an airtight container up to 2 weeks.

Lemon Knots

Tarralucci

Makes 40

Every Italian bakery in Brooklyn, New York, made these refreshing Sicilian lemon cookies when I was growing up. I like to serve them with iced tea.

If the weather is hot and humid, the icing may refuse to firm up at room temperature. In that case, store the cookies in the refrigerator.

4 cups all-purpose flour

4 teaspoons baking powder

1 cup sugar

½ cup solid vegetable shortening

3 large eggs

½ cup milk

2 tablespoons lemon juice

2 teaspoons grated lemon zest

Icing

1½ cups confectioner's sugar

1 tablespoon freshly squeezed lemon juice

2 teaspoons grated lemon zest

Milk

1. Sift together the flour and baking powder onto a piece of wax paper.

2. In a large bowl, with an electric mixer at medium speed, beat the sugar and shortening until light and fluffy, about 2 minutes. Beat in the eggs one at a time until well blended. Stir in the milk, lemon juice, and zest. Scrape the sides of the bowl. Stir in the dry ingredients until smooth, about 2 minutes. Cover with plastic wrap and refrigerate at least 1 hour.

3. Preheat the oven to 350°F. Have ready 2 large baking sheets. Pinch off a piece of dough the size of a golf ball. Lightly roll the dough into a 6-inch rope. Tie the rope into a knot. Place the knot on an ungreased baking sheet. Continue making the knots and placing them about 1 inch apart on the sheets.

4. Bake the cookies 12 minutes or until firm when pressed on top but not browned. Have ready 2 wire cooling racks.

5. Transfer the baking sheets to the racks. Let the cookies cool 5 minutes on the baking sheets, then transfer them to the wire racks to cool completely.

6. Combine the confectioner's sugar, lemon juice, and zest in a large bowl. Add milk 1 teaspoon at a time and stir until the mixture forms a thin icing with the consistency of heavy cream.

7. Dip the tops of the cookies in the icing. Place them on a rack until the icing is hardened. Store in airtight containers up to 3 days.

Spice Cookies

Bicciolani

Makes 75

In caffès in Turin you can order barbajada, a combination of half coffee and half hot chocolate. It would be perfect with these thin, buttery spice cookies.

1 cup (2 sticks) unsalted butter, at room temperature

1 cup sugar

1 egg yolk

2 cups all-purpose flour

½ teaspoon salt

1 teaspoon ground cinnamon

⅛ teaspoon freshly grated nutmeg

⅛ teaspoon ground cloves

1. Preheat the oven to 350°F. Grease a 15 × 10 × 1– inch jelly roll pan.

2. In a bowl, stir together the flour, salt, and spices.

3. In a large electric mixer bowl, beat the butter, sugar, and egg yolk on medium speed until light and fluffy, about 2 minutes. Reduce the speed to low and stir in the dry ingredients until thoroughly blended, about 2 minutes more.

4. Crumble the dough into the prepared pan. With your hands, firmly press the dough out into an even layer. With the back of a fork, make shallow ridges in the top of the dough.

5. Bake 25 to 30 minutes or until lightly browned. Transfer the pan to a wire cooling rack. Cool 10 minutes. Then cut the dough into 2 × 1–inch cookies.

6. Cool completely in the pan. Store at room temperature in an airtight container up to 2 weeks.

Wafer Cookies

Pizzelle

Makes about 2 dozen

Many families in central and southern Italy are proud of their pizzelle irons, beautifully crafted forms traditionally used to make these pretty wafers. Some irons are embossed with the original owner's initials, while others have silhouettes such as a couple toasting each other with a glass of wine. They were once a typical wedding gift.

Though charming, these old fashioned irons are heavy and unwieldy on today's stoves. An electric pizzelle press, similar to a waffle iron, does an efficient and quick job of turning out these cookies.

When they are freshly made, pizzelle are pliable and can be molded into cone, tube, or cup shapes. They can be filled with whipped cream, ice cream, cannoli cream, or fruit. They cool and crisp in no time, so you must work quickly and carefully to shape them. Of course, they are good flat as well.

1¾ cups unbleached all-purpose flour

1 teaspoon baking powder

Pinch of salt

3 large eggs

⅔ cup sugar

1 tablespoon pure vanilla extract

1 stick (½ cup) unsalted butter, melted and cooled

1. Preheat the pizzelle maker according to the manufacturer's directions. In a bowl, stir together the flour, baking powder, and salt.

2. In a large bowl, beat the eggs, sugar, and vanilla with an electric mixer on medium speed until thick and light, about 4 minutes. Beat in the butter. Stir in the dry ingredients until just blended, about 1 minute.

3. Place about 1 tablespoon of the batter in the center of each pizzelle mold. (The exact amount will depend on the design of the mold.) Close the cover and bake until lightly golden. This will depend on the maker and how long the mold has been heating. Check it carefully after 30 seconds.

4. When the pizzelle are golden, slide them off the molds with a wooden or plastic spatula. Let cool flat on a wire rack. Or, to make cookie cups, bend each pizzelle into the curve of a wide coffee or dessert cup. To make cannoli shells, shape them around cannoli tubes or a wooden dowel.

5. When the pizzelle are cool and crisp, store them in an airtight container until ready to use. These last for several weeks.

Variation: *Anise*: Substitute 1 tablespoon anise extract and 1 tablespoon anise seeds for the vanilla. *Orange or Lemon*: Add 1 tablespoon grated fresh orange or lemon zest to the egg mixture. *Rum or Almond*: Stir in 1 tablespoon rum or almond extract instead of the vanilla. *Nut*: Stir in $1/4$ cup of nuts ground to a very fine powder along with the flour.

Sweet Ravioli

Ravioli Dolci

Makes 2 dozen

Jam fills these crisp dessert ravioli. Any flavor will do, as long as it has a thick consistency so that it will stay in place and not ooze out of the dough as it bakes. This was a favorite recipe of my father, who perfected it from his memories of the cookies his mother used to make.

1¾ cup all-purpose flour

½ cup potato or corn starch

½ teaspoon salt

½ cup (1 stick) unsalted butter, at room temperature

½ cup sugar

1 large egg

2 tablespoons rum or brandy

1 teaspoon grated lemon zest

1 teaspoon pure vanilla extract

1 cup thick sour cherry, raspberry, or apricot jam

1. In a large bowl, sift together the flour, starch, and salt.

2. In a large bowl with an electric mixer, beat the butter with the sugar until light and fluffy, about 2 minutes. Beat in the egg, rum, zest, and vanilla. On low speed, stir in the dry ingredients.

3. Divide the dough in half. Shape each half into a disk. Wrap each separately in plastic and refrigerate 1 hour up to overnight.

4. Preheat the oven to 350°F. Grease 2 large baking sheets.

5. Roll out the dough to a $1/8$-inch thickness. With a fluted pastry or pasta cutter, cut the dough into 2-inch squares. Arrange the squares about 1 inch apart on the prepared baking sheets. Place $1/2$ teaspoon of the jam in the center of each square. (Do not use more jam, or the filling will leak out as it bakes.)

6. Roll out the remaining dough to a $1/8$-inch thickness. Cut the dough into 2-inch squares.

7. Cover the jam with the dough squares. Press the edges all around with a fork to seal in the filling.

8. Bake 16 to 18 minutes, or until lightly browned. Have ready 2 wire cooling racks.

9. Transfer the baking sheets to the racks. Let the cookies cool 5 minutes on the baking sheets, then transfer them to the wire racks to cool completely. Sprinkle with confectioner's sugar. Store in an airtight container up to 1 week.

"Ugly-but-Good" Cookies

Brutti ma Buoni

Makes 2 dozen

"Ugly but good" is the meaning of the name of these Piedmontese cookies. The name is only half-true: The cookies are not ugly, but they are good. The technique for making these is unusual. The cookie batter is cooked in a saucepan before it is baked.

3 large egg whites, at room temperature

Pinch of salt

1½ cups sugar

1 cup unsweetened cocoa powder

1¼ cups hazelnuts, toasted, peeled, and coarsely chopped (see How To Toast and Skin Nuts)

1. Preheat the oven to 300°F. Grease 2 large baking sheets.

2. In a large bowl, with an electric mixer at medium speed, beat the egg whites and salt until foamy. Increase the speed to high and gradually add the sugar. Beat until soft peaks form when the beaters are lifted.

3. On low speed, mix in the cocoa. Stir in the hazelnuts.

4. Scrape the mixture into a large heavy saucepan. Cook over medium heat, stirring constantly with a wooden spoon, until the mixture is shiny and smooth, about 5 minutes. Be careful that it does not scorch.

5. Immediately drop the hot batter by tablespoonfuls onto the prepared baking sheets. Bake 30 minutes or until firm and slightly cracked on the surface.

6. While the cookies are still hot, transfer them to a rack to cool, using a thin-blade metal spatula. Store in an airtight container up to 2 weeks.

Jam Spots

Biscotti di Marmellata

Makes 40

Chocolate, nuts, and jam are a winning combination in these tasty cookies. They are always a hit on Christmas cookie trays.

¾ cup (1½ sticks) unsalted butter, at room temperature

½ cup sugar

½ teaspoon salt

3 ounces bittersweet chocolate, melted and cooled

2 cups all-purpose flour

¾ cup finely chopped almonds

½ cup thick seedless raspberry jam

1. Preheat the oven to 350°F. Grease 2 large baking sheets.

2. In a large bowl, with an electric mixer on medium speed, beat the butter, sugar, and salt until light and fluffy, about 2 minutes.

Add the melted chocolate and beat until well blended, scraping the sides of the bowl. Stir in the flour until smooth.

3. Place the nuts in a shallow bowl. Shape the dough into 1-inch balls. Roll the balls in the nuts, pressing lightly so they will adhere. Place the balls about $1^1/_2$ inches apart on the prepared baking sheets.

4. With the handle end of a wooden spoon, poke a deep hole in each ball of dough, molding the dough around the handle to maintain the round shape. Place about $^1/_4$ teaspoon jam in each cookie. (Do not add more jam, as it may melt and leak out when the cookies bake.)

5. Bake the cookies 18 to 20 minutes, or until the jam is bubbling and the cookies are lightly browned. Have ready 2 wire cooling racks.

6. Transfer the baking sheets to the racks. Let the cookies cool 5 minutes on the baking sheets, then transfer them to the wire racks to cool completely. Store in an airtight container up to 2 weeks.

Double-Chocolate Nut Biscotti

Biscotti al Cioccolato

Makes 4 dozen

These rich biscotti have chocolate in the dough, both melted and in chunks. I have never seen them in Italy, but they are similar to what I have tasted in coffee bars here.

2½ cups all-purpose flour

2 teaspoons baking powder

½ teaspoon salt

3 large eggs, at room temperature

1 cup sugar

1 teaspoon pure vanilla extract

6 ounces bittersweet chocolate, melted and cooled

6 tablespoons (½ stick plus 2 tablespoons) unsalted butter, melted and cooled

1 cup walnuts, coarsely chopped

1 cup chocolate chips

1. Place a rack in the center of the oven. Preheat the oven to 300°F. Grease and flour 2 large baking sheets.

2. In a large bowl, sift together the flour, baking powder, and salt.

3. In a large bowl, with an electric mixer at medium speed, beat the eggs, sugar, and vanilla until foamy and light, about 2 minutes. Stir in the chocolate and butter until blended. Add the flour mixture and stir until smooth, about 1 minute more. Stir in the nuts and chocolate chips.

4. Divide the dough in half. With moistened hands, shape each piece into a 12 × 3-inch log on the prepared baking sheet. Bake for 35 minutes or until the logs are firm when pressed in the center. Remove the pan from the oven, but do not turn off the heat. Let cool 10 minutes.

5. Slide the logs onto a cutting board. Cut the logs into $1/2$-inch-thick slices. Lay the slices on the baking sheet. Bake for 10 minutes or until the cookies are lightly toasted.

6. Have ready 2 large cooling racks. Transfer the baking sheets to the racks. Let the cookies cool 5 minutes on the baking sheets,

then transfer them to the racks to cool completely. Store in an airtight container up to 2 weeks.

Chocolate Kisses

Baci di Cioccolato

Makes 3 dozen

Chocolate and vanilla "kisses" are a favorite in Verona, home of Romeo and Juliet, where they are made in a variety of combinations.

1 2/3 cups all-purpose flour

1/3 cup unsweetened Dutch-process cocoa powder, sifted

1/4 teaspoon salt

1 cup (2 sticks) unsalted butter, at room temperature

1/2 cup confectioner's sugar

1 teaspoon pure vanilla extract

1/2 cup finely chopped toasted almonds (see How To Toast and Skin Nuts)

Filling

2 ounces semisweet or bittersweet chocolate, chopped

2 tablespoons unsalted butter

⅓ cup almonds, toasted and finely chopped

1. In a large bowl, sift together the flour, cocoa, and salt.

2. In a large bowl, with an electric mixer at medium speed, beat the butter and sugar until light and fluffy, about 2 minutes. Beat in the vanilla. Stir in the dry ingredients and the almonds until blended, about 1 minute more. Cover with plastic and chill in the refrigerator 1 hour up to overnight.

3. Preheat the oven to 350°F. Have ready 2 ungreased baking sheets. Roll teaspoonfuls of the dough into ¾-inch balls. Place the balls 1 inch apart on the baking sheets. With your fingers, press the balls to flatten them slightly. Bake the cookies until firm but not browned, 10 to 12 minutes. Have ready 2 large cooling racks.

4. Transfer the baking sheets to the racks. Let the cookies cool 5 minutes on the baking sheets, then transfer them to the racks to cool completely.

5. Bring about 2 inches of water to a simmer in the bottom half of a double boiler or a small saucepan. Place the chocolate and the butter in the top half of the double boiler or in a small heatproof bowl that fits comfortably over the saucepan. Place the bowl

over the simmering water. Let stand uncovered until the chocolate is softened. Stir until smooth. Stir in the almonds.

6. Spread a small amount of the filling mixture on the bottom of one cookie. Place a second cookie bottom-side down on the filling and press together lightly. Place the cookies on a wire rack until the filling is set. Repeat with the remaining cookies and filling. Store in an airtight container in the refrigerator up to 1 week.

No-Bake Chocolate "Salame"

Salame del Cioccolato

Makes 32 cookies

Crunchy chocolate nut slices that require no baking are a specialty of Piedmont. Other cookies can be substituted for the amaretti, if you prefer, such as vanilla or chocolate wafers, graham crackers, or shortbread. These are best made a few days ahead, to allow the flavors to blend. If you prefer not use the liqueur, substitute a spoonful of orange juice.

18 amaretti cookies

⅓ cup sugar

⅓ cup unsweetened cocoa powder

½ cup (1 stick) unsalted butter, softened

1 tablespoon grappa or rum

⅓ cup chopped walnuts

1. Place the cookies in a plastic bag. Crush the cookies with a rolling pin or heavy object. There should be about ¾ cup of crumbs.

2. Place the crumbs in a large bowl. With a wooden spoon, stir in the sugar and cocoa. Add the butter and grappa. Stir until the dry ingredients are moistened and blended. Stir in the walnuts.

3. Place a 14-inch sheet of plastic wrap on a flat surface. Pour the dough mixture onto the plastic wrap. Shape the dough into an 8 × 2 1/2–inch log. Roll the log in the plastic wrap, folding the ends over to enclose it completely. Refrigerate the log at least 24 hours and up to 3 days.

4. Cut the log into 1/4-inch-thick slices. Serve chilled. Store the cookies in an airtight plastic container in the refrigerator up to 2 weeks.

Prato Biscuits

Biscotti di Prato

Makes about 4½ dozen

In the town of Prato in Tuscany, these are the classic biscotti to dip in vin santo, the great dessert wine of the region. Eaten plain, they are rather dry, so do provide a beverage for dunking them.

2½ cups all-purpose flour

1½ teaspoons baking powder

1 teaspoon salt

4 large eggs

¾ cup sugar

1 teaspoon grated lemon zest

1 teaspoon grated orange zest

1 teaspoon pure vanilla extract

1 cup toasted almonds (see How To Toast and Skin Nuts)

1. Place a rack in the center of the oven. Preheat the oven to 325°F. Grease and flour a large baking sheet.

2. In a medium bowl, sift together the flour, baking powder, and salt.

3. In a large bowl with an electric mixer, beat the eggs and sugar on medium speed until light and foamy, about 3 minutes. Beat in the lemon and orange zests and vanilla. On low speed, stir in the dry ingredients, then stir in the almonds.

4. Lightly dampen your hands. Shape the dough into two 14 × 2-inch logs. Place the logs on the prepared baking sheet several inches apart. Bake for 30 minutes or until firm and golden.

5. Remove the baking sheet from the oven and reduce the oven heat to 300°F. Let the logs cool on the baking sheet for 20 minutes.

6. Slide the logs onto a cutting board. With a large heavy chef's knife, cut the logs on the diagonal into $1/2$-inch-thick slices. Lay the slices on the baking sheet. Bake 20 minutes or until lightly golden.

7. Transfer the cookies to wire racks to cool. Store in an airtight container.

Umbrian Fruit and Nut Biscotti

Tozzetti

Makes 80

Made without fat, these cookies keep a long time in an airtight container. The flavor actually improves, so plan to make them several days before serving them.

3 cups all-purpose flour

½ cup cornstarch

2 teaspoons baking powder

3 large eggs

3 egg yolks

2 tablespoons Marsala, vin santo, or sherry

1 cup sugar

1 cup raisins

1 cup almonds

¼ cup chopped candied orange peel

¼ cup chopped candied citron

1 teaspoon anise seeds

1. Preheat the oven to 350°F. Grease 2 large baking sheets.

2. In a medium bowl, sift together the flour, cornstarch, and baking powder.

3. In a large bowl with an electric mixer, beat together the eggs, yolks, and Marsala. Add the sugar and beat until well blended, about 3 minutes. Stir in the dry ingredients, the raisins, almonds, peel, citron and anise seeds until blended. The dough will be stiff. If necessary, turn the dough out onto a countertop and knead it until blended.

4. Divide the dough into quarters. Dampen your hands with cool water and shape each quarter into a 10-inch log. Place the logs 2 inches apart on the prepared baking sheets.

5. Bake the logs 20 minutes or until they feel firm when pressed in the center and are golden brown around the edges. Remove the logs from the oven but leave the oven on. Let the logs cool 5 minutes on the baking sheets.

6. Slide the logs onto a cutting board. With a large chef's knife, cut them into $1/2$-inch-thick slices. Place the slices on the baking sheets and bake 10 minutes or until lightly toasted.

7. Have ready 2 large cooling racks. Transfer the cookies to the racks. Let cool completely. Store in an airtight container up to 2 weeks.

Lemon Nut Biscotti

Biscotti al Limone

Makes 48

Lemon and almonds flavor these biscotti.

1½ cups all-purpose flour

1 teaspoon baking powder

¼ teaspoon salt

½ cup (1 stick) unsalted butter, at room temperature

½ cup sugar

2 large eggs, at room temperature

2 teaspoons freshly grated lemon zest

1 cup toasted almonds, coarsely chopped

1. Place a rack in the center of the oven. Preheat the oven to 350°F. Grease and flour a large baking sheet.

2. In a bowl, sift together the flour, baking powder, and salt.

3. In a large bowl with an electric mixer, beat the butter and sugar until light and fluffy, about 2 minutes. Beat in the eggs one at a time. Add the lemon zest, scraping the inside of the bowl with a rubber spatula. Gradually stir in the flour mixture and the nuts until blended.

4. Divide the dough in half. With moistened hands, shape each piece into a 12 × 2–inch log on the prepared baking sheet. Bake for 20 minutes or until the logs are lightly browned and firm when pressed in the center. Remove the pan from the oven, but do not turn off the heat. Let the logs cool 10 minutes on the baking sheet.

5. Slide the logs onto a cutting board. Cut the logs into $1/2$-inch-thick slices. Place the slices on the baking sheet. Bake for 10 minutes or until the cookies are lightly toasted.

6. Have ready 2 large cooling racks. Transfer the cookies to the racks. Let cool completely. Store in an airtight container up to 2 weeks.

Walnut Biscotti

Biscotti di Noce

Makes about 80

Olive oil can be used for baking in a wide range of recipes. Use a mild-flavored extra-virgin olive oil. It complements many types of nuts and citrus fruits. Here is a biscotti recipe I developed for an article in the Washington Post about baking with olive oil.

2 cups all-purpose flour

1 teaspoon baking powder

1 teaspoon salt

2 large eggs, at room temperature

⅔ cup sugar

½ cup extra-virgin olive oil

½ teaspoon grated lemon zest

2 cups toasted walnuts (see How To Toast and Skin Nuts)

1. Preheat the oven to 325°F. Grease 2 large baking sheets.

2. In a large bowl, combine the flour, baking powder, and salt.

3. In another large bowl, whisk the eggs, sugar, oil, and lemon zest until well blended. With a wooden spoon, stir in the dry ingredients just until blended. Stir in the walnuts.

4. Divide the dough into four pieces. Shape the pieces into 12 × 1 1/2-inch logs, placing them several inches apart on the prepared baking sheets. Bake for 20 to 25 minutes or until lightly browned. Remove from the oven, but do not turn it off. Let the cookies cool on the baking sheets 10 minutes.

5. Slide the logs onto a cutting board. With a large heavy knife, cut the logs diagonally into 1/2-inch slices. Lay the slices on the baking sheets and return the sheets to the oven. Bake 10 minutes or until toasted and golden.

6. Have ready 2 large cooling racks. Transfer the cookies to the racks. Let cool completely. Store in an airtight container up to 2 weeks.

Almond Macaroons

Amaretti

Makes 3 dozen

In southern Italy, these are made by grinding up both sweet and bitter almonds. Bitter almonds, which come from a particular variety of almond tree, are not sold in the United States. They have a flavor component similar to cyanide, a lethal poison, so they are not approved for commercial use. The closest we can come to the correct flavor is commercial almond paste and a little almond extract. Do not confuse almond paste with marzipan, which is similar, but has a higher sugar content. Buy the almond paste sold in cans for best flavor. If you can't find it, ask at your local bakery to see if they will sell you some.

These cookies stick, so I bake them on nonstick baking mats known as Silpat. The mats never need greasing, are easy to clean, and reusable. You can find them at good kitchen supply stores. If you don't have the mats, the baking pans can be lined with parchment paper or aluminum foil.

1 (8-ounce) can almond paste, crumbled

1 cup sugar

2 large egg whites, at room temperature

¼ teaspoon almond extract

36 candied cherries or whole almonds

1. Preheat the oven to 350°F. Line 2 large baking sheets with parchment paper or aluminum foil.

2. Crumble the almond paste into a large bowl. With an electric mixer on low speed, beat in the sugar until blended. Add the egg whites and almond extract. Increase the speed to medium and beat until very smooth, about 3 minutes.

3. Scoop up 1 tablespoon of the batter and lightly roll it into a ball. Dampen your fingertips with cool water if necessary to prevent sticking. Place the balls about one inch apart on the prepared baking sheet. Press a cherry or almond into the top of the dough.

4. Bake 18 to 20 minutes or until the cookies are lightly browned. Let cool briefly on the baking sheet.

5. With a thin metal spatula, transfer the cookies to wire racks to cool completely. Store the cookies in airtight containers. (If you want to keep these cookies for more than a day or two, freeze

them to maintain their soft texture. They can be eaten directly from the freezer.)

Pine Nut Macaroons

Biscotti di Pinoli

Makes 40

I have made many variations of these cookies over the years. This version is my favorite because it is made with both almond paste and ground almonds for both flavor and texture and has the added rich flavor of toasted pine nuts (pignoli).

1 (8-ounce) can almond paste

⅓ cup finely ground blanched almonds

2 large egg whites

1 cup confectioner's sugar, plus more for decorating

2 cups pine nuts or slivered almonds

1. Place a rack in the center of the oven. Preheat the oven to 350°F. Grease a large baking sheet.

2. In a large bowl, crumble the almond paste. With an electric mixer on medium speed, beat in the almonds, egg whites, and 1 cup of confectioner's sugar until smooth.

3. Scoop up a tablespoon of the batter. Roll the batter in the pine nuts, covering it completely and forming a ball. Place the ball on the prepared baking sheet. Repeat with the remaining ingredients, placing the balls about 1 inch apart.

4. Bake 18 to 20 minutes or until lightly browned. Place the baking sheet on a cooling rack. Let the cookies cool 2 minutes on the baking sheet.

5. Transfer the cookies to racks to cool completely. Dust with confectioner's sugar. Store in an airtight container in the refrigerator up to 1 week.

Hazelnut Bars

Nocciolate

Makes 6 dozen

These tender, crumbly bars are packed with nuts. They barely hold together and melt in the mouth. Serve them with chocolate ice cream.

2 ⅓ cups all-purpose flour

1½ cups peeled, toasted hazelnuts, finely chopped (see How To Toast and Skin Nuts)

1½ cups sugar

½ teaspoon salt

1 cup (2 sticks) unsalted butter, melted and cooled

1 large egg plus 1 egg yolk, beaten

1. Place a rack in the center of the oven. Preheat the oven to 350°F. Grease a 15 × 10 × 1–inch jelly roll pan.

2. In a large bowl with a wooden spoon, stir together the flour, nuts, sugar, and salt. Add the butter and stir until evenly

moistened. Add the eggs. Stir until well blended and the mixture holds together.

3. Pour the mixture into the prepared pan. Firmly pat it out into an even layer.

4. Bake 30 minutes or until golden brown. While still hot, cut into 2 × 1-inch rectangles.

5. Let cool 10 minutes in the pan. Transfer the cookies to large racks to cool completely.

Walnut Butter Cookies

Biscotti di Noce

Makes 5 dozen

Nutty and buttery, these crescent-shaped cookies from Piedmont are perfect for Christmas. Though they are often made with hazelnuts, I like to use walnuts. Almonds can also be substituted.

These cookies can be made entirely in the food processor. If you don't have one, grind the nuts and sugar in a blender or nut grinder, then stir in the remaining ingredients by hand.

1 cup walnut pieces

⅓ cup sugar plus 1 cup more for rolling the cookies

2 cups all-purpose flour

1 cup (2 sticks) unsalted butter, at room temperature

1. Preheat oven to 350°F. Grease and flour 2 large baking sheets.

2. In a food processor, combine the walnuts and sugar. Process until the nuts are finely chopped. Add the flour and process until blended.

3. Add the butter a little at a time and pulse to blend. Remove the dough from the container and squeeze it together with your hands.

4. Pour the remaining 1 cup of sugar into a shallow bowl. Pinch off a piece of dough the size of a walnut and form it into a ball. Shape the ball into a crescent, tapering the ends. Gently roll the crescent in sugar. Place the crescent on a prepared baking sheet. Repeat with the remaining dough and sugar, placing each cookie about 1 inch apart.

5. Bake 15 minutes or until lightly browned. Place the baking sheets on wire racks to cool 5 minutes.

6. Transfer the cookies to the racks to cool completely. Store in an airtight container up to 2 weeks.

Rainbow Cookies

Biscotti Tricolori

Makes about 4 dozen

Though I have never seen them in Italy, these "rainbow," or tricolored, cookies with a chocolate glaze are a favorite at Italian and other bakeries in the United States. Unfortunately, they are often colored garishly and can be dry and tasteless.

Try this recipe and you will see how good these cookies can be. They are a bit fussy to make, but the results are very pretty and delicious. If you prefer not to use food coloring, the cookies will still be attractive. For convenience, it is best to have three identical baking pans. But you can still make the cookies with only one pan if you bake one batch of dough at a time. The finished cookies keep well in the refrigerator.

8 ounces almond paste

1½ cups (3 sticks) unsalted butter

1 cup sugar

4 large eggs, separated

¼ teaspoon salt

2 cups unbleached all-purpose flour

10 drops red food coloring, or to taste (optional)

10 drops green food coloring, or to taste (optional)

½ cup apricot preserves

½ cup seedless raspberry jam

1 (6-ounce) package semisweet chocolate chips

1. Preheat the oven to 350°F. Grease three 13 × 9 × 2– inch identical baking pans. Line the pans with wax paper and grease the paper.

2. Crumble the almond paste into a large mixer bowl. Add the butter, ½ cup of the sugar, the egg yolks, and salt. Beat until light and fluffy. Stir in the flour just until blended.

3. In another large bowl, with clean beaters, beat the egg whites on medium speed until foamy. Gradually beat in the remaining sugar. Increase the speed to high. Continue beating until the egg whites form soft peaks when the beaters are lifted.

4. With a rubber spatula, fold $1/3$ of the whites into the yolk mixture to lighten it. Gradually fold in the remaining whites.

5. Scoop $1/3$ of the batter into one bowl, and another $1/3$ into another bowl. If using the food coloring, fold the red into one bowl and the green into the other.

6. Spread each bowl of batter into a separate prepared pan, smoothing it out evenly with a spatula. Bake the layers 10 to 12 minutes, until the cake is just set and very lightly colored around the edges. Let cool in the pan for 5 minutes, then lift the layers onto cooling racks, leaving the wax paper attached. Let cool completely.

7. Using the paper to lift one layer, invert the cake and place it paper-side up on a large tray. Carefully peel off the paper. Spread with a thin layer of the raspberry jam.

8. Set a second layer paper-side up on top of the first. Remove the paper and spread the cake with the apricot jam.

9. Place the remaining layer paper-side up on top. Peel off the paper. With a large heavy knife and a ruler as a guide, trim the edges of the cake to make the layers straight and even all around.

10. Bring about 2 inches of water to a simmer in the bottom half of a double boiler or a small saucepan. Place the chocolate chips in the top half of the double boiler or in a small heatproof bowl that fits comfortably over the saucepan. Place the bowl over the simmering water. Let stand uncovered until the chocolate is softened. Stir until smooth. Pour the melted chocolate on top of the cake layers and spread it smooth with a spatula. Refrigerate until the chocolate is just beginning to set, about 30 minutes. (Don't let it get too hard, or it will crack when you cut it.)

11. Remove the cake from the refrigerator. Using a ruler or other straight edge as a guide, cut the cake lengthwise into 6 strips by first cutting it into thirds, then cutting each third in half. Cut crosswise into 5 strips. Chill the cut cake in the pan in the refrigerator until the chocolate is firm. Serve or transfer the cookies to an airtight container and store in the refrigerator. These keep well for several weeks.

Christmas Fig Cookies

Cuccidati

Makes 18 large cookies

I can't imagine Christmas without these cookies. For many Sicilians, making them is a family project. The women mix and roll the dough, while the men chop and grind the filling ingredients. The children decorate the filled cookies. They are traditionally cut into many fanciful shapes resembling birds, leaves, or flowers. Some families make dozens of them to give away to friends and neighbors.

Dough

2½ cups all-purpose flour

⅓ cup sugar

2 teaspoons baking powder

½ teaspoon salt

6 tablespoons unsalted butter

2 large eggs, at room temperature

1 teaspoon pure vanilla extract

Filling

2 cups moist dried figs, stems removed

½ cup raisins

1 cup walnuts, toasted and chopped

½ cup chopped semisweet chocolate (about 2 ounces)

⅓ cup honey

¼ cup orange juice

1 teaspoon orange zest

1 teaspoon ground cinnamon

⅛ teaspoon ground cloves

Assembly

1 egg yolk beaten with 1 teaspoon water

Colored candy sprinkles

1. Prepare the dough: In a large bowl, combine the flour, sugar, baking powder, and salt. Cut in the butter, using an electric

mixer or pastry blender, until the mixture resembles coarse crumbs.

2. In a bowl, whisk the eggs and vanilla. Add the eggs to the dry ingredients, stirring with a wooden spoon until the dough is evenly moistened. If the dough is too dry, blend in a little cold water a few drops at a time.

3. Gather the dough into a ball and place it on a sheet of plastic wrap. Flatten it into a disk and wrap well. Refrigerate at least 1 hour or overnight.

4. Prepare the filling: In a food processor or meat grinder, grind the figs, raisins, and nuts until coarsely chopped. Stir in the remaining ingredients. Cover and refrigerate if not using within the hour.

5. To assemble the pastries, preheat the oven to 375°F. Grease two large baking sheets.

6. Cut the dough into 6 pieces. On a lightly floured surface, roll each piece into a log about 4 inches long.

7. With a floured rolling pin, roll one log into a 9 × 5-inch rectangle. Trim the edges.

8. Spoon a ³/₄-inch strip of the filling lengthwise slightly to one side of the center of the rolled out dough. Fold one long side of the dough over to the other and press the edges together to seal. Cut the filled dough crosswise into 3 even pieces.

9. With a sharp knife, cut slits ³/₄-inch long at ¹/₂-inch intervals through the filling and dough. Curving them slightly to open the slits and reveal the fig filling, place the pastries one inch apart on the baking sheets.

10. Brush the pastry with the egg wash. Drizzle with candy sprinkles if desired. Repeat with the remaining ingredients.

11. Bake the cookies 20 to 25 minutes or until golden brown.

12. Cool the cookies on wire racks. Store in an airtight container in the refrigerator up to 1 month.

Almond Brittle

Croccante or Torrone

Makes 10 to 12 servings

Sicilians make these sweets with pine nuts, pistachios, or sesame seeds in place of the almonds. A lemon is perfect to smooth out the hot syrup.

Vegetable oil

2 cups sugar

¼ cup honey

2 cups almonds (10 ounces)

1 whole lemon, washed and dried

1. Brush a marble surface or a metal baking sheet with neutral-flavored vegetable oil.

2. In a medium saucepan, combine the sugar and honey. Cook over medium-low heat, stirring occasionally, until the sugar begins to melt, about 20 minutes. Bring to a simmer and cook without stirring 5 minutes more or until the syrup is clear.

3. Add the nuts and cook until the syrup is amber-colored, about 3 minutes. Carefully pour the hot syrup onto the prepared surface, using the lemon to smooth the nuts to a single layer. Let cool completely. When the brittle is cool and hard, after about 30 minutes, slide a thin metal spatula underneath it. Lift the brittle and break it into $1^{1}/_{2}$-inch pieces. Store in airtight containers at room temperature.

Sicilian Nut Rolls

Mostaccioli

Makes 64 cookies

At one time these cookies were made with mosto cotto, concentrated wine grape juice. Today's cooks use honey.

Dough

3 cups all-purpose flour

½ cup sugar

1 teaspoon salt

½ cup shortening

4 tablespoons (½ stick) unsalted butter, at room temperature

2 large eggs

2 to 3 tablespoons cold milk

Filling

1 cup toasted almonds

1 cup toasted walnuts

½ cup toasted and skinned hazelnuts

¼ cup sugar

¼ cup honey

2 teaspoons orange zest

¼ teaspoon ground cinnamon

Confectioner's sugar

1. In a large bowl, combine the flour, sugar, and salt. Cut in the shortening and butter until the mixture resembles coarse crumbs.

2. In a small bowl, whisk the eggs with two tablespoons of the milk. Add the mixture to the dry ingredients, stirring until the dough is evenly moistened. If needed, blend in a little more milk.

3. Gather the dough into a ball and place it on a sheet of plastic wrap. Flatten it into a disk and wrap well. Refrigerate 1 hour up to overnight.

4. Process the nuts and sugar in a food processor. Process until fine. Add the honey, zest, and cinnamon, and process until

blended. Preheat the oven to 350°F. Grease 2 large baking sheets.

5. Divide the dough into 4 pieces. Roll out one piece between two sheets of plastic wrap to form a square slightly larger than 8 inches. Trim the edges and cut the dough into 2-inch squares. Place a heaping teaspoon of the filling along one side of each square. Roll up the dough to enclose the filling completely. Place seam-side down on the baking pan. Repeat with the remaining dough and filling, placing the cookies 1 inch apart.

6. Bake 18 minutes or until the cookies are lightly browned. Transfer the cookies to wire racks to cool. Store in a tightly sealed container up to 2 weeks. Sprinkle with confectioner's sugar before serving.

Sponge Cake

Pan di Spagna

Makes two 8- or 9-inch layers

This classic and versatile Italian sponge cake works well with fillings such as fruit preserves, whipped cream, pastry cream, ice cream, or ricotta cream. The cake also freezes well, so it is convenient to have on hand for quick desserts.

Butter for the pan

6 large eggs, at room temperature

$2/3$ cup sugar

$1\frac{1}{2}$ teaspoons pure vanilla extract

1 cup sifted all-purpose flour

1. Place the rack in the center of the oven. Preheat the oven to 375°F. Butter two 8- or 9-inch layer cake pans. Line the bottom of the pans with circles of waxed paper or parchment paper. Butter the paper. Dust the pans with flour and tap out the excess.

2. In a large bowl with an electric mixer, begin beating the eggs on low speed. Slowly add the sugar, gradually increasing the mixer speed to high. Add the vanilla. Beat the eggs until thick and pale yellow, about 7 minutes.

3. Place the flour in a fine-mesh strainer. Shake about one-third of the flour over the egg mixture. Gradually and very gently fold in the flour with a rubber spatula. Repeat, adding the flour in 2 additions and folding it in until there are no streaks.

4. Spread the batter evenly in the prepared pans. Bake 20 to 25 minutes or until the cakes spring back when pressed lightly in the center and the top is lightly browned. Have ready 2 cooling racks. Cool the cakes 10 minutes in the pans on the wire racks.

5. Invert the cakes onto the racks and remove the pans. Carefully peel off the paper. Let cool completely. Serve immediately or cover with an inverted bowl and store at room temperature up to 2 days.

Citrus Sponge Cake

Torta di Agrumi

Serves 10 to 12

Olive oil gives this cake a distinctive flavor and texture. Use a mild olive oil or the flavor could be intrusive. Because it does not contain butter, milk, or other dairy products, this cake is good for people who cannot eat those foods.

This is a big cake, though it is very light and airy. To bake it, you will need a 10-inch tube pan with a removable bottom—the kind used for angel cakes.

A little bit of cream of tartar, available in the spice section of most supermarkets, helps to stabilize the egg whites in this large cake.

2¼ cups plain cake flour (not self-rising)

1 tablespoon baking powder

1 teaspoon salt

6 large eggs, separated, at room temperature

1¼ cups sugar

1½ teaspoons orange zest

1½ teaspoons grated lemon zest

¾ cup freshly squeezed orange juice

½ cup extra-virgin olive oil

1 teaspoon pure vanilla extract

¼ teaspoon cream of tartar

1. Place the oven rack in the lower third of the oven. Preheat the oven to 325°F. In a large bowl, sift together the flour, baking powder, and salt.

2. In a large bowl with an electric mixer, beat the egg yolks, 1 cup of the sugar, the orange and lemon zests, the orange juice, oil, and vanilla extract until smooth, about 5 minutes. With a rubber spatula, fold the liquid into the dry ingredients.

3. In another large bowl with clean beaters, beat the egg whites on medium speed until foamy. Gradually add the remaining ¼ cup of sugar and the cream of tartar. Increase the speed to high. Beat until soft peaks form when the beaters are lifted, about 5 minutes. Fold the whites into the batter.

4. Scrape the batter into an ungreased 10-inch tube pan with a removable bottom. Bake 55 minutes or until the cake is golden brown and a toothpick inserted in the center comes out clean.

5. Place the pan upside down on a cooling rack and let the cake cool completely. Run a thin-blade knife around the inside of the pan to loosen the cake. Lift out the cake and the bottom of the pan. Slide the knife under the cake and remove the pan bottom. Serve immediately, or cover with an overturned bowl and store at room temperature up to 2 days.

Lemon Olive-Oil Cake

Torta di Limone

Makes 8 servings

A light, lemony cake from Puglia that is always a pleasure to have on hand.

1½ cups plain cake flour (not self-rising)

1½ teaspoons baking powder

½ teaspoon salt

3 large eggs, at room temperature

1 cup sugar

⅓ cup olive oil

1 teaspoon pure vanilla extract

1 teaspoon grated lemon zest

¼ cup freshly squeezed lemon juice

1. Place the rack in the lowest third of the oven. Preheat oven to 350°F. Grease a 9-inch springform pan.

2. In a large bowl, sift together the flour, baking powder, and salt.

3. Break the eggs into a large electric mixer bowl. Beat on medium speed until thick and pale yellow, about 5 minutes. Slowly add in the sugar and beat 3 minutes more. Slowly add the oil. Beat one minute more. Add the vanilla and lemon zest.

4. With a rubber spatula, fold in the dry ingredients in three additions, alternating with the lemon juice in two additions.

5. Scrape the batter into the prepared pan. Bake 35 to 40 minutes or until the cake is golden brown and springs back when pressed in the center.

6. Turn the pan upside down on a wire rack. Let cool completely. Run a knife around the outside rim and remove it. Serve immediately, or cover with an overturned bowl and store at room temperature up to 2 days.

Marble Cake

Torta Marmorata

Makes 8 to 10 servings

Breakfast is not given a lot of attention in Italy. Eggs and cereal are rarely eaten, and most Italians get by on coffee with toast or perhaps a plain cookie or two. Hotel breakfasts often overcompensate for foreign tastes with a lavish variety of cold meats, cheeses, fruit, eggs, yogurt, bread, and pastries. At one hotel in Venice, I spotted a magnificent marble cake, one of my personal favorite cakes, proudly displayed on a cake stand. It was heavenly with a cup of cappuccino, and I would have enjoyed it equally at teatime. The waiter told me the cake was delivered fresh daily from a local bakery where it was a specialty. This is my version, inspired by the one in Venice.

1½ cups plain cake flour (not self-rising)

1½ teaspoons baking powder

½ teaspoon salt

3 large eggs, at room temperature

1 cup sugar

⅓ cup vegetable oil

1 teaspoon pure vanilla extract

¼ teaspoon almond extract

½ cup milk

2 ounces bittersweet or semisweet chocolate, melted and cooled

1. Place the oven rack in the lowest third of the oven. Preheat the oven to 325°F. Grease and flour a 10-inch tube pan and tap out the excess flour.

2. In a large bowl, sift together the flour, baking powder, and salt.

3. In another large bowl, with an electric mixer, beat the eggs on medium speed until thick and pale yellow, about 5 minutes. Slowly beat in the sugar a tablespoon at a time. Continue beating 2 minutes more.

4. Gradually beat in the oil and extracts. Fold in the flour in 3 additions, alternately adding the milk in two additions.

5. Remove about 1½ cups of the batter and place it in a small bowl. Set aside. Scrape the remaining batter into the prepared pan.

6. Fold the melted chocolate into the reserved batter. Place large spoonfuls of the chocolate batter on top of the batter in the pan. To swirl the batter, hold a table knife with the tip down. Insert the knife blade down through batter, running it gently all around the pan at least 2 times.

7. Bake 40 minutes or until the cake is golden brown and a toothpick comes out clean when inserted in the center. Let cool on a rack 10 minutes.

8. Invert the cake onto the rack and remove the pan. Turn the cake right-side up on another rack. Let cool completely. Serve immediately, or cover with an inverted bowl and store at room temperature up to 2 days.

Rum Cake

Baba au Rhum

Makes 8 to 10 servings

According to a popular story, this cake was invented by a Polish king who found his babka, a Polish yeast cake, too dry and poured a glass of rum on it. His creation was named baba, after Ali Baba of the Arabian Nights. How it became popular in Naples is not certain, but it has been for some time.

Because it is leavened with yeast rather than baking powder, baba has a spongy texture, perfect for absorbing the rum syrup. Some versions are baked in miniature muffin pans, while others have a pastry cream filling. I like to serve this with strawberries and whipped cream on the side—not typical, but delicious, and makes a lovely presentation.

1 package (2½ teaspoons) active dry yeast or instant yeast

¼ cup warm milk (100° to 110°F)

6 large eggs

2⅔ cups all-purpose flour

3 tablespoons sugar

½ teaspoon salt

¾ cup (1½ sticks) unsalted butter, at room temperature

Syrup

2 cups sugar

2 cups water

2 (2-inch) strips lemon zest

¼ cup rum

1. Grease a 10-inch tube pan.

2. Sprinkle the yeast over the warm milk. Let stand until creamy, about 1 minute, then stir until dissolved.

3. In a large mixing bowl, with an electric mixer on medium speed, beat the eggs until foamy, about 1 minute. Beat in the flour, sugar, and salt. Add the yeast and butter and beat until well blended, about 2 minutes

4. Scrape the dough into the prepared pan. Cover with plastic wrap and let stand in a warm place 1 hour or until the dough has doubled in volume.

5. Place a rack in the center of the oven. Preheat the oven to 400°F. Bake the cake 30 minutes or until it is golden and a toothpick inserted in the center comes out clean.

6. Invert the cake onto a cooling rack. Remove the pan and let cool for 10 minutes.

7. To make the syrup, combine the sugar, water, and lemon zest in a medium saucepan. Bring the mixture to a boil and stir until the sugar is dissolved, about 2 minutes. Remove the lemon zest. Stir in the rum. Set aside $1/4$ cup of the syrup.

8. Return the cake to the pan. With a fork, poke holes all over the surface. Slowly spoon the syrup over the cake while both are still hot. Let cool completely in the pan.

9. Just before serving, invert the cake onto a serving plate Drizzle with the remaining syrup. Serve immediately. Store covered with an overturned bowl at room temperature up to 2 days.

Grandmother's Cake

Torta della Nonna

Makes 8 servings

I couldn't decide whether to include this recipe—called torta della nonna—with the tarts or with the cakes; however, because Tuscans call it a torta, I include it with the cakes. It consists of two layers of pastry filled with a thick pastry cream. I don't know whose grandmother invented it, but everyone loves her cake. There are many variations, some including lemon flavoring.

1 cup milk

3 large egg yolks

⅓ cup sugar

1½ teaspoons pure vanilla extract

2 tablespoons all-purpose flour

2 tablespoons orange liqueur or rum

Dough

1⅔ cup all-purpose flour

½ cup sugar

1 teaspoon baking powder

½ teaspoon salt

½ cup (1 stick) unsalted butter, at room temperature

1 large egg, lightly beaten

1 teaspoon pure vanilla extract

1 egg yolk beaten with 1 teaspoon water, for egg wash

2 tablespoons pine nuts

Confectioner's sugar

1. In a medium saucepan, heat the milk over low heat until bubbles form around the edges. Remove from the heat.

2. In a medium bowl, whisk the egg yolks, sugar, and vanilla until pale yellow, about 5 minutes. Whisk in the flour. Gradually add the hot milk, whisking constantly. Transfer the mixture to the saucepan and cook over medium heat, stirring constantly, until boiling. Reduce the heat and simmer for 1 minute. Scrape the mixture into a bowl. Stir in the liqueur. Place a piece of plastic

wrap directly on the surface of the custard to prevent a skin from forming. Refrigerate 1 hour up to overnight.

3. Place the rack in the center of the oven. Preheat the oven to 350°F. Grease a 9 × 2–inch round cake pan.

4. Prepare the dough: In a large bowl, stir together the flour, sugar, baking powder, and salt. With a pastry blender, cut in the butter until the mixture resembles coarse crumbs. Add the egg and vanilla and stir until a dough forms. Divide the dough in half.

5. Scatter half of the dough evenly in the bottom of the prepared pan. Press the dough into the bottom of the pan and $1/2$ inch up the sides. Spread the chilled custard over the center of the dough, leaving a 1-inch border around the edge.

6. On a lightly floured surface, roll out the remaining dough to a $9^1/_2$-inch circle. Place the dough over the filling. Press the edges of the dough together to seal. Brush the egg wash over the top of the cake. Sprinkle with the pine nuts. With a small knife, make several slits in the top to allow steam to escape.

7. Bake 35 to 40 minutes, or until golden brown on top. Let cool in the pan on a rack for 10 minutes.

8. Invert the cake onto the rack, then invert onto another rack to cool completely. Sprinkle with confectioner's sugar before serving. Serve immediately, or wrap the cake in plastic wrap and refrigerate up to 8 hours. Wrap and store in the refrigerator.

Apricot Almond Cake

Torta di Albicocche e Mandorle

Makes 8 servings

Apricots and almonds are very compatible flavors. If you can't find fresh apricots, substitute peaches or nectarines.

Topping

⅔ cup sugar

¼ cup water

12 to 14 apricots or 6 to 8 peaches, halved, pitted, and cut into ¼-inch-thick slices

Cake

1 cup all-purpose flour

1 teaspoon baking powder

½ teaspoon salt

½ cup almond paste

2 tablespoons unsalted butter

⅔ cup sugar

½ teaspoon pure vanilla extract

2 large eggs

⅔ cup milk

1. Prepare the topping: Place the sugar and water in a small heavy saucepan. Cook over medium heat, stirring occasionally, until the sugar is completely dissolved, about 3 minutes. When the mixture begins to boil, stop stirring and cook until the syrup starts to brown around the edges. Then gently swirl the pan over the heat until the syrup is an even golden brown, about 2 minutes more.

2. Protecting your hand with a pot holder, immediately pour the caramel into a 9 × 2–inch round cake pan. Tilt the pan to coat the bottom evenly. Let the caramel cool until set, about 5 minutes.

3. Place the oven rack in the center of the oven. Preheat the oven to 350°F. Arrange the sliced fruit, overlapping them slightly, in circles on top of the caramel.

4. Combine the flour, baking powder, and salt in a fine-mesh strainer set over a piece of wax paper. Sift the dry ingredients onto the paper.

5. In a large electric mixer bowl, beat the almond paste, butter, sugar, and vanilla until fluffy, about 4 minutes. Beat in the eggs one at a time, scraping the side of the bowl. Continue beating until smooth and well blended, about 4 minutes more.

6. With the mixer on low speed, stir in 1/3 of the flour mixture. Add 1/3 of the milk. Add the remaining flour mixture and milk in two more additions in the same way, ending with the flour. Stir just until smooth.

7. Pour the batter over the fruit. Bake 40 to 45 minutes or until the cake is golden and a toothpick inserted in the center comes out clean.

8. Let the cake cool in the pan on a wire rack 10 minutes. Run a thin metal spatula around the inside of the pan. Invert the cake onto a serving plate (the fruit will be on top) and let cool completely before serving. Serve immediately, or cover with an inverted bowl and store at room temperature up to 24 hours.

Summer Fruit Torte

Torta dell'Estate

Makes 8 servings

Soft stone fruits such as plums, apricots, peaches, and nectarines are ideal for this torte. Try making it with a combination of fruits.

12 to 16 prune plums or apricots, or 6 medium peaches or nectarines, halved, pitted, and cut into ½-inch slices

1 cup all-purpose flour

1 teaspoon baking powder

½ teaspoon salt

½ cup (1 stick) unsalted butter, at room temperature

⅔ cup plus 2 tablespoons sugar

1 large egg

1 teaspoon grated lemon zest

1 teaspoon pure vanilla extract

Confectioner's sugar

1. Place the rack in the center of the oven. Preheat the oven to 350°F. Grease a 9-inch springform pan.

2. In a large bowl, mix together the flour, baking powder, and salt.

3. In another large bowl, beat the butter with $2/3$ cup of the sugar until light and fluffy, about 3 minutes. Beat in the egg, lemon zest, and vanilla until smooth. Add the dry ingredients and stir just until blended, about 1 minute more.

4. Scrape the batter into the prepared pan. Arrange the fruit, overlapping it slightly, on top in concentric circles. Sprinkle with the remaining 2 tablespoons of sugar.

5. Bake 45 to 50 minutes or until the cake is golden brown and a toothpick inserted in the center comes out clean.

6. Let the cake cool in the pan on a wire rack 10 minutes, then remove the rim of the pan. Let the cake cool completely. Sprinkle with confectioner's sugar before serving. Serve immediately, or cover with an overturned bowl and store at room temperature up to 24 hours.

Autumn Fruit Torte

Torta del Autunno

Makes 8 servings

Apples, pears, figs, or plums are good in this simple cake. The batter forms a top layer that does not quite cover the fruit, allowing it to peek through the surface of the cake. I like to serve it slightly warm.

1½ cups all-purpose flour

1 teaspoon baking powder

½ teaspoon salt

2 large eggs

1 cup sugar

1 teaspoon pure vanilla extract

4 tablespoons unsalted butter, melted and cooled

2 medium apples or pears, peeled, cored, and sliced into thin wedges

Confectioner's sugar

1. Place the rack in the center of the oven. Preheat the oven to 350°F. Grease and flour a 9-inch springform cake pan. Tap out the excess flour.

2. In a bowl, stir together the flour, baking powder, and salt.

3. In a large bowl, beat the eggs with the sugar and vanilla until blended, about 2 minutes. Beat in the butter. Stir in the flour mixture until just blended, about 1 minute more.

4. Spread half of the batter in the prepared pan. Cover with the fruits. Drop the remaining batter on top by spoonfuls. Spread the batter evenly over the fruits. The layer will be thin. Don't be concerned if the fruit is not completely covered.

5. Bake 30 to 35 minutes or until the cake is golden brown and a toothpick inserted in the center comes out clean.

6. Let the cake cool 10 minutes in the pan on a wire rack. Remove the rim of the pan. Cool the cake completely on the rack. Serve warm or at room temperature with a sprinkle of confectioner's sugar. Store covered with a large inverted bowl at room temperature up to 24 hours.

Polenta and Pear Cake

Dolce di Polenta

Makes 8 servings

Yellow cornmeal adds a pleasant texture and warm golden color to this rustic cake from the Veneto.

1 cup all-purpose flour

⅓ cup finely ground yellow cornmeal

1 teaspoon baking powder

½ teaspoon salt

¾ cup (1½ sticks) unsalted butter, softened

¾ cup plus 2 tablespoons sugar

1 teaspoon pure vanilla extract

½ teaspoon grated lemon zest

2 large eggs

⅓ cup milk

1 large ripe pear, cored and thinly sliced

1. Place a rack in the center of the oven. Preheat the oven to 350°F. Grease and flour a 9-inch springform pan. Tap out the excess flour.

2. In a large bowl, sift together the flour, cornmeal, baking powder, and salt.

3. In a large bowl with an electric mixer, beat the butter, gradually adding $3/4$ cup of the sugar until light and fluffy, about 3 minutes. Beat in the vanilla and lemon zest. Beat in the eggs one at time, scraping the sides of the bowl. On low speed, stir in half of the dry ingredients. Add the milk. Stir in the remaining dry ingredients just until smooth, about 1 minute.

4. Spread the batter in the prepared pan. Arrange the pear slices on top, overlapping them slightly. Sprinkle the pear with the remaining 2 tablespoons of sugar.

5. Bake 45 minutes or until the cake is golden brown and a toothpick inserted in the center comes out clean.

6. Cool the cake in the pan 10 minutes on a wire rack. Remove the pan rim and cool the cake completely on the rack. Serve

immediately, or cover with a large inverted bowl and store at room temperature up to 24 hours.

Ricotta Cheesecake

Torta di Ricotta

Makes 12 servings

I like to think of this as an American-style Italian cheesecake. It is a large cake, though the flavor is delicate, with lemon zest and cinnamon. This cake is baked in a water bath so that it cooks evenly. The base of the pan is wrapped in foil to prevent the water from seeping into the pan.

1¼ cups sugar

⅓ cup all-purpose flour

½ teaspoon ground cinnamon

3 pounds whole or part-skim ricotta

8 large eggs

2 teaspoons pure vanilla extract

2 teaspoons grated lemon zest

1. Place a rack in the center of the oven. Preheat the oven to 350°F. Grease and flour a 9-inch springform pan. Tap out the excess

flour. Place the pan on a 12-inch square of heavy-duty aluminum foil. Mold the foil tightly around the base and about 2 inches up the sides of the pan so that water cannot seep in.

2. In a medium bowl, stir together the sugar, flour, and cinnamon.

3. In a large mixing bowl, whisk the ricotta until smooth. Beat in the eggs, vanilla, and lemon zest until well blended. (For a smoother texture, beat the ingredients with an electric mixer or process them in a food processor.) Whisk in the dry ingredients just until blended.

4. Pour the batter into the prepared pan. Set the pan in a large roasting pan and place it in the oven. Carefully pour hot water to a depth of 1 inch in the roasting pan. Bake $1^1/_2$ hours or until the top of the cake is golden and a toothpick inserted 2 inches from the center comes out clean.

5. Turn off the oven and prop the door open slightly. Let the cake cool in the turned off oven 30 minutes. Remove the cake from the oven and remove the foil wrapping. Cool to room temperature in the pan on a wire rack.

6. Serve at room temperature or refrigerate and serve slightly chilled. Store covered with an inverted bowl in the refrigerator up to 3 days.

Sicilian Ricotta Cake

Cassata

Makes 10 to 12 servings

Cassata is the glory of Sicilian desserts. It consists of two layers of pan di Spagna (Sponge Cake) filled with sweetened, flavored ricotta. The whole cake is frosted with two icings, one of tinted almond paste and the other flavored with lemon. Sicilians decorate the cake with glistening candied fruits and almond paste cutouts so that it looks like something out of a fairy tale.

Originally served only at Easter time, cassata is now found at celebrations throughout the year.

    2 Sponge Cake layers

1 pound whole or part-skim ricotta

½ cup confectioner's sugar

1 teaspoon pure vanilla extract

¼ teaspoon ground cinnamon

½ cup chopped semisweet chocolate

2 tablespoons chopped candied orange peel

Icing

4 ounces almond paste

2 or 3 drops green food coloring

2 egg whites

¼ teaspoon grated lemon zest

1 tablespoon fresh lemon juice

2 cups confectioner's sugar

Candied or dried fruits, such as cherries, pineapple, or citron

1. Prepare the sponge cake, if necessary. Then, in a large bowl with a wire whisk, beat the ricotta, sugar, vanilla, and cinnamon until smooth and creamy. Fold in the chocolate and orange peel.

2. Place one cake layer on a serving plate. Spread the ricotta mixture on top. Place the second cake layer over the filling.

3. For the decoration, crumble the almond paste into a food processor fitted with the steel blade. Add one drop of the food coloring. Process until evenly tinted a light green, adding more

color if needed. Remove the almond paste and shape it into a short thick log.

4. Cut the almond paste into 4 lengthwise slices. Place one slice between two sheets of wax paper. With a rolling pin, flatten it into a narrow ribbon 3 inches long and $1/8$-inch thick. Unwrap and trim off any rough edges, reserving the scraps. Repeat with the remaining almond paste. The ribbons should be about the same width as the height of the cake. Wrap the almond paste ribbons end to end all around the sides of the cake, overlapping the ends slightly.

5. Gather the scraps of almond paste and reroll them. Cut into decorative shapes, such as stars, flowers, or leaves, with cookie cutters.

6. Prepare the icing: Whisk the egg whites, lemon zest, and juice. Add the confectioner's sugar and stir until smooth.

7. Spread the icing evenly over the top of the cake. Decorate the cake with the almond paste cutouts and the candied fruits. Cover with a large overturned bowl and refrigerate until serving time, up to 8 hours. Store leftovers covered in the refrigerator up to 2 days.

Ricotta Crumb Cake

Sbriciolata di Ricotta

Makes 8 servings

Brunch, a very American meal, is fashionable right now in Milan and other cities in northern Italy. This is my version of the ricotta-filled crumb cake I ate at brunch at a caffè not far from the Piazza del Duomo in the heart of Milan.

2½ cups all-purpose flour

½ teaspoon salt

½ teaspoon ground cinnamon

¾ cup (1½ sticks) unsalted butter

⅔ cup sugar

1 large egg

Filling

1 pound whole or part-skim ricotta

¼ cup sugar

1 teaspoon grated lemon zest

1 large egg, beaten

¼ cup raisins

Confectioner's sugar

1. Place a rack in the center of the oven. Preheat the oven to 350°F. Grease and flour a 9-inch springform pan. Tap out the excess flour.

2. In a large bowl, stir together the flour, salt, and cinnamon.

3. In a large bowl, with an electric mixer at medium speed, beat together the butter and sugar until light and fluffy, about 3 minutes. Beat in the egg. On low speed, stir in the dry ingredients until the mixture is blended and forms a firm dough, about 1 minute more.

4. Prepare the filling: Stir together the ricotta, sugar, and lemon zest until blended. Add the egg and stir well. Stir in the raisins.

5. Crumble ⅔ of the dough into the prepared pan. Pat the crumbs firmly to form the bottom crust. Spread with the ricotta mixture, leaving a ½-inch border all around. Crumble the remaining dough over the top, scattering the crumbs evenly.

6. Bake 40 to 45 minutes or until the cake is golden brown and a toothpick inserted in the center comes out clean. Let cool in the pan on a rack 10 minutes.

7. Run a thin metal spatula around the inside of the pan. Remove the pan rim and cool the cake completely. Sprinkle with confectioner's sugar before serving. Store covered with a large inverted bowl in the refrigerator up to 2 days.

Easter Wheat-Berry Cake

La Pastiera

Wheat berries add a slightly chewy texture to this traditional Neapolitan Easter cake. This was my father's mother's recipe, which she brought with her from Procida, an island off the coast of Naples. Neapolitans love this dessert, and you will find it in bakeries and restaurants in the area all year round. Both the crust and the filling are flavored with cinnamon and orange-flower water, a delicate essence made from orange blossoms that is frequently used in southern Italian desserts. It can be found in many gourmet stores, spice shops, and ethnic markets. Substitute fresh orange juice if you cannot find it. Hulled wheat is often found in Italian markets and natural food stores, or try the mail order sources.

Dough

3 cups all-purpose flour

½ teaspoon ground cinnamon

½ teaspoon salt

¾ cup (1½ sticks) unsalted butter, softened

1 cup confectioner's sugar

1 large egg

2 large egg yolks

2 teaspoons orange-flower water

Filling

4 ounces hulled wheat (about ½ cup)

½ teaspoon salt

½ cup (1 stick) unsalted butter, softened

1 teaspoon grated orange zest

1 pound (2 cups) whole or part-skim ricotta

4 large eggs, at room temperature

⅔ cup sugar

3 tablespoons orange-flower water

1 teaspoon ground cinnamon

½ cup very finely chopped candied citron

½ cup very finely chopped candied orange peel

Confectioner's sugar

1. Prepare the dough: In a large bowl, stir together the flour, cinnamon, and salt.

2. In a large bowl with an electric mixer on medium speed, beat the butter and confectioner's sugar until light and fluffy, about 3 minutes. Add the egg and yolks and beat until smooth. Beat in the orange-flower water. Add the dry ingredients and stir just until blended, about 1 minute more.

3. Shape $1/4$ of the dough into a disk. Make a second disk with the remaining dough. Wrap each piece in plastic wrap and chill 1 hour up to overnight.

4. Prepare the filling: Place the wheat in a large bowl, add cold water to cover, and let soak overnight in the refrigerator. Drain the wheat.

5. Place the soaked wheat in a medium saucepan with cold water to cover. Add the salt and bring to a simmer over medium heat. Cook, stirring occasionally, until the wheat is tender, 20 to 30 minutes. Drain, and place in a large bowl. Stir in the butter and orange zest. Let cool.

6. Place the rack in the lower third of the oven. Preheat the oven to 350°F. Grease and flour a 9 × 3– inch springform pan. In a large bowl, whisk together the ricotta, eggs, sugar, orange-flower water, and cinnamon. Beat until blended. Stir in the wheat mixture, citron, and candied orange peel.

7. Roll out the larger piece of dough to a 16-inch circle. Drape the dough over the rolling pin. Using the pin to lift it, fit the dough into the pan, flattening out any wrinkles against the inside of the pan. Scrape the filling onto the dough and smooth the top.

8. Roll out the smaller piece of dough to a 10-inch circle. With a fluted pastry cutter, cut the dough into $1/2$-inch-wide strips. Lay the strips across the filling in a lattice pattern. Press the ends of the strips against the dough on the sides of the pan. Trim the dough, leaving $1/2$ inch of excess all around the rim, and fold the edge of the crust over the ends of the lattice strips. Press firmly to seal.

9. Bake 1 hour 10 minutes or until the cake is golden brown on top and a toothpick inserted in the center comes out clean.

10. Let the cake cool in the pan on a rack 15 minutes. Remove the rim of the pan and let the cake cool completely on a wire rack.

Just before serving, sprinkle with confectioner's sugar. Store covered with an inverted bowl in the refrigerator up to 3 days.

Chocolate Hazelnut Cake

Torta Gianduja

Makes 8 to 10 servings

Chocolate and hazelnut, a favorite combination in Piedmont, is known as gianduja (pronounced gyan-doo-ya). You will find many candies made or filled with gianduja, gelato flavored with gianduja, and the most famous gianduja of all, Nutella, a creamy jarred chocolate hazelnut spread that Italian kids prefer to peanut butter. Gianduja is also the name of the stock character in commedia dell'arte who represents Turin, the capital city of Piedmont.

This Piedmontese cake is dark, dense, and extremely rich.

6 ounces semisweet or bittersweet chocolate

1 2/3 cups hazelnuts, toasted and skinned (see How To Toast and Skin Nuts)

1/2 cup (1 stick) unsalted butter, at room temperature

1 cup sugar

5 large eggs, separated

Pinch of salt

Glaze

6 ounces semisweet or bittersweet chocolate, chopped

2 tablespoons unsalted butter

1. In the bottom half of a double boiler or in a medium saucepan, bring 2 inches of water to a simmer. Place the chocolate in the top half of the double boiler or in a bowl that will sit comfortably over the saucepan. Let the chocolate stand until softened, about 5 minutes. Stir until smooth. Let cool slightly.

2. Place the oven rack in the center of the oven. Preheat the oven to 350°F. Grease a 9 × 2–inch round cake pan.

3. In a food processor or blender, finely chop the hazelnuts. Set aside 2 tablespoons.

4. In a large bowl, with an electric mixer at medium speed, beat the butter with the sugar until light and fluffy, about 3 minutes. Add the egg yolks and beat until smooth. With a rubber spatula, stir in the chocolate and hazelnuts.

5. In a large clean bowl with clean beaters, whip the egg whites and salt on medium speed until foamy, about 1 minute. Increase the speed to high and beat until soft peaks form, about 5

minutes. With a rubber spatula, gently fold a large spoonful of the whites into the chocolate mixture to lighten it. Then gradually fold in the remainder. Scrape the batter into the prepared pan and smooth the surface. Bake 55 to 60 minutes, or until the cake is firm around the edge but slightly moist in the center.

6. Let cool in the pan for 15 minutes on a wire rack. Then unmold the cake onto a rack, invert onto another rack, and let cool completely right-side up.

7. Prepare the glaze: Bring about 2 inches of water to a simmer in the bottom half of a double boiler or a small saucepan. Place the chocolate and the butter in the top half of the double boiler or in a small heatproof bowl that fits comfortably over the saucepan. Place the bowl over the simmering water. Let stand uncovered until the chocolate is softened. Stir until smooth.

8. Place the cake on a cake rack set over a large piece of wax paper. Pour the glaze over the cake and spread it evenly over the sides and top with a long metal spatula.

9. Sprinkle the remaining 2 tablespoons of chopped nuts around the edge of the cake. Let stand in a cool place until the glaze is set.

10. Serve at room temperature. Store covered with a large inverted bowl in the refrigerator up to 3 days.

Chocolate Almond Cake

Torta Caprese

Makes 8 servings

I am not sure how this delicate cake became a specialty of Capri, but for me it is a great memento of my visits there. Serve it with whipped cream.

8 ounces semisweet or bittersweet chocolate

1 cup (2 sticks) unsalted butter, at room temperature

1 cup sugar

6 large eggs, separated, at room temperature

1½ cups almonds, very finely ground

Pinch of salt

Unsweetened cocoa powder

1. In the bottom half of a double boiler or in a medium saucepan, bring 2 inches of water to a simmer. Place the chocolate in the top half of the double boiler or in a heatproof bowl that will sit comfortably over the saucepan. Let the chocolate stand until softened, about 5 minutes. Stir until smooth. Let cool slightly.

2. Place the oven rack in the center of the oven. Preheat the oven to 350°F. Grease and flour a 9-inch round cake pan. Tap out the excess flour.

3. In a large bowl with an electric mixer at medium speed, beat the butter with $3/4$ cup of the sugar until light and fluffy, about 3 minutes. Add the egg yolks one at a time, beating well after each addition. With a rubber spatula, stir in the chocolate and the almonds.

4. In a large clean bowl with clean beaters, beat the egg whites with the salt on medium speed until foamy. Increase the speed to high and beat in the remaining $1/4$ cup of sugar. Continue to beat until the egg whites are glossy and hold soft peaks when the beaters are lifted, about 5 minutes.

5. Fold about $1/4$ of the whites into the chocolate mixture to lighten it. Gradually fold in the remaining whites.

6. Scrape the batter into the prepared pan. Bake 45 minutes or until the cake is set around the edge but soft and moist in the center and a toothpick inserted in the center comes out covered with chocolate. Let cool in the pan on a rack 10 minutes.

7. Run a thin metal spatula around the inside of the pan. Invert the cake onto a plate. Turn it right-side up onto a cooling rack. Let cool completely, then dust with cocoa powder. Serve at room temperature. Store covered with a large inverted bowl in the refrigerator up to 3 days.

Chocolate Orange Torte

Torta di Cioccolatta all' Arancia

Makes 8 servings

Chocolate and orange make an excellent combination in this unusual cake from Liguria. Be sure to use moist, flavorful candied orange peel for this cake.

6 ounces bittersweet or semisweet chocolate

6 large eggs, at room temperature, separated

2/3 cup sugar

2 tablespoons orange liqueur

1 2/3 cup walnuts, toasted and very finely chopped (see How To Toast and Skin Nuts)

1/3 cup finely chopped candied orange peel

Confectioner's sugar

1. Place the rack in the lower third of the oven. Preheat the oven to 350°F. Grease and flour a 9-inch springform pan, tapping out the excess flour.

2. In the bottom half of a double boiler or in a medium saucepan, bring 2 inches of water to a simmer. Place the chocolate in the top half of the double boiler or in a bowl that will sit comfortably over the saucepan. Let the chocolate stand until softened, about 5 minutes. Stir until smooth.

3. In a large bowl, with an electric mixer at medium speed, beat the egg yolks and $1/3$ cup of the sugar until thick and pale yellow, about 5 minutes. Beat in the orange liqueur. Stir in the chocolate, nuts, and orange peel.

4. In a large clean mixer bowl, beat the egg whites on medium speed until foamy. Gradually beat in the remaining $1/3$ cup of sugar. Increase the speed and beat until the whites are glossy and soft peaks form, about 5 minutes. With a rubber spatula, fold $1/3$ of the beaten whites into the chocolate mixture to lighten it. Gradually fold in the remainder.

5. Scrape the batter into the prepared pan. Bake 45 minutes or until the cake is set around the edge but still slightly moist when a toothpick is inserted in the center.

6. Cool the cake completely in the pan on a wire rack. Run a thin metal spatula around the inside of the pan to release it. Remove the rim and place the cake on a serving plate. Just before serving, sprinkle the cake with confectioner's sugar. Serve at room temperature. Store covered with a large inverted bowl in the refrigerator up to 3 days.

www.ingramcontent.com/pod-product-compliance
Lightning Source LLC
Chambersburg PA
CBHW071820080526

44589CB00012B/866